Surprised by God

Surprised by God

Teaching Reflection through the Parables

Christina R. Zaker

ROWMAN & LITTLEFIELD
Lanham • Boulder • New York • London

Published by Rowman & Littlefield
An imprint of The Rowman & Littlefield Publishing Group, Inc.
4501 Forbes Boulevard, Suite 200, Lanham, Maryland 20706
www.rowman.com

6 Tinworth Street, London SE11 5AL, United Kingdom

Copyright © 2020 by The Rowman & Littlefield Publishing Group, Inc.

All rights reserved. No part of this book may be reproduced in any form or by any electronic or mechanical means, including information storage and retrieval systems, without written permission from the publisher, except by a reviewer who may quote passages in a review.

British Library Cataloguing in Publication Information Available

Library of Congress Cataloging-in-Publication Data

Names: Zaker, Christina, 1967– author.
Title: Surprised by God : teaching reflection through the parables / Christina Zaker.
Description: Lanham : Rowman & Littlefield, [2020] | Includes bibliographical references and index. | Summary: "Zaker introduces foundational elements of theological reflection including definitions and guidance through various methods. Offering a lens for reflection based on the unique way Jesus' parables surprise and invite listeners to collaborate in the kingdom of God, the book foregrounds the importance of honest spiritual reflection"—Provided by publisher.
Identifiers: LCCN 2020034070 (print) | LCCN 2020034071 (ebook) | ISBN 9781538143902 (cloth) | ISBN 9781538143926 (epub)
Subjects: LCSH: Theology—Methodology. | Jesus Christ—Parables.
Classification: LCC BR118 .Z345 2020 (print) | LCC BR118 (ebook) | DDC 230.01—dc23
LC record available at https://lccn.loc.gov/2020034070
LC ebook record available at https://lccn.loc.gov/2020034071

Contents

Acknowledgments	vii
Introduction	1
1 Breathing Deeply: Noticing God in the Midst of Life	5
2 Cultivating the Heart: Carving Out the Space for Reflective Practice	21
3 The Wisdom of the Parables: Developing Ears that Can Hear and Eyes that Can See	49
4 Exploring Parable as a Lens for Reflection: Key Frameworks for Reflective Practice	63
5 Connecting: Reflective Practice, Solidarity, and the Spiritual Life	87
6 Practicing Reflection: Reflective Practice through the Lens of Parables	103
Epilogue: Finding Hope in Family during COVID-19	125
Appendix A—Theological Reflection in Parabolic Mode	135
Appendix B—High School Service Journal	139
Bibliography	141
Index	145
About the Author	147

Acknowledgments

It is with deep gratitude and love that I acknowledge the enduring support and encouragement of my husband, Christopher. Our life together has been truly blessed and I thank him for helping to shape our stories, some of which have made it onto these pages. I thank Micah, Evelyn, Joshua, and Josephine—our children—for their joy, laughter, wisdom, and encouragement throughout life and especially during the months of writing this project.

I am especially grateful to Fr. Edward Foley, OFM Cap who served as the director of my doctoral thesis project that started this parabolic journey. Much of my work here began in that original thesis project. My colleagues at Catholic Theological Union have been profoundly inspiring, especially Kathleen Martin for generously spending hours reading and editing drafts of each chapter and so many other colleagues whose friendship and encouragement sustained me on this journey. I am also grateful to my students who continuously shape my understanding of theological reflection and ministry. Thank you for sharing your stories and your wisdom.

Introduction

While celebrating mass on October 13, 2014, Pope Francis said, "Our God is a God of surprises," he went on to invite his listeners to consider these questions: "Am I open to the God of surprises? Am I a person who stands still, or a person on a journey?" These insights are at the heart of this project. The parables Jesus told were familiar stories filled with surprising invitations to understand the reign of God and they provide a unique lens for reflecting on our journey of faith. *Surprised by God: Teaching Reflection through the Lens of Parables* explores what it means to reflect on life, to ask ourselves if we are open to the God of surprises, and to consider the steps we take on our journey.

Surprised by God is an important book at this moment. The digital realm is inundated with social media posts and YouTube stories capturing life's important (and sometimes not so important) moments. These are posted at lightning speed, yet rarely do people pause and consider why they are sharing, "liking," or posting something in the first place. The habit to pause and notice the motivation behind our actions is a skill that needs honing. There is a hunger to connect and to share our story; however, the turn inward to reflect on our place in that story is not familiar territory. Our recent COVID-19 crisis has everyone around the world experiencing "social distancing" and "sheltering at home" and perhaps this will bear fruit in our ability to unpack life's experiences in a reflective and transformative way. But even for ministers who are skilled in the reflective arts, the demands on their time and the speed at which they attempt to respond to those with whom they minister means that carving out the space for reflective practice is often seen as an "extracurricular" and falls to the bottom of the priority list. The art of reflection is a skill that has been stifled by distractions in every direction.

This book aims to respond by helping readers cultivate reflective spaces in their hearts and in their communities in an accessible and adaptable way.

The genesis for this project began in the work for my 2012 Ecumenical Doctorate in Ministry at Catholic Theological Union which focused on parables as a lens for theological reflection. This work, coupled with over 30 years of ministry leading college students, post grad volunteers, and now graduate students in theological reflection has shaped the lessons learned and stories shared in this book. Theological reflection is an important tool in ministry and for life. Socrates is credited with saying, "The unexamined life is not worth living." Theological reflection open to God's surprising nearness offers not only a way to examine life, but also provides the tools to encourage the transformation necessary to join God on the journey.

I hope to provide theology students, as well as any person interested in honing their reflective skills, the tools to develop a reflective habit in daily life. Reflection is not a retreat, or something to be checked off our to-do list; this is a habit to be honed and explored over time. The tools discussed in this book create a new way to engage in life that leans on theology and, more specifically, the parables as a guide. It offers a unique way to reflect on our stories and teach people (ministry students, everyday seekers, and street theologians) to reflect theologically and to be *parabled*: to be reflective practitioners alive to and challenged by the surprising movement of God in their midst.

Surprised by God provides an in-depth look at the foundational elements of theological reflection. The first chapter will engage the reader in reflective activities that cultivate a sacramental imagination open to the God of surprises. This chapter builds the foundation that reflective practice aims to attune our hearts to values and beliefs bigger than ourselves. The second chapter defines theological reflection, looks briefly at a number of methods employed in ministerial contexts, and offers suggestions on how to cultivate the space and habitus of reflection. The conviction that theological reflection is an important tool for any person as they navigate life is at the heart of the best practices shared throughout chapter 2.

Chapter 3 turns to look at the parables of Jesus. Here we explore how parables offer a lens for reflection that draws its framework from the unique ways Jesus' parables surprise and invite his listeners to collaborate in the reign of God. We will examine my favorite parable as an example of the pattern and explore how the parables offer a provocative lens for theological reflection. Chapter 4 lays out what I see as the lens of parables. Here we will discuss the important questions to ask to move theological reflection through dialogue to action. The reality of intercultural and interreligious settings of today means that our reflective practices must be more adaptable and fluid. As Edward Foley, OFM Cap notes, "The shifting spiritual terrain and even hybridity of believing in the twenty-first century requires . . . a certain methodological agility here" (2015, 48). The lens of parables provides a scaffold that is simple enough to be layered over other patterns of reflective practice, but provocative enough to challenge practitioners to further critical depths of belief and action.

Chapter 5 points out the importance of reflection as spiritual practice and suggests that theological reflection through the lens of parable does the important work of turning this practice toward questions of justice and solidarity. Chapter 6 provides examples of how the lens of parable can be adapted for a variety of settings. Academic, ministerial, and even secular adaptations are highlighted to show the lens of parable is an adept framework for reflection and growth.

I firmly believe that theological reflection is not only a tool for theologians but is also a spiritual practice for any person. This book encourages each of us to ponder our deepest values and how we become a part of the bigger story of our world. Theological reflection through the lens of parable lays us open to the God of surprises and challenges us to respond. Jesus' parables are often framed with phrases like "Whoever has ears to hear, let them hear" (Luke 8:8). This sense of learning to truly hear and see and notice God at work in the world is at the heart of theological reflection and it is my hope that this book makes theological reflection accessible so that all may have "ears that will hear."

Chapter 1

Breathing Deeply

Noticing God in the Midst of Life

Before we begin, I want you to pause, take a deep breath, and close your eyes for 15 seconds. Take another deep breath and just allow a sense of being embraced by love and hope permeate your breathing. Know that wherever you are as you read this book, you and countless others around the world are sharing a breath at the same time. As I write, I too am thinking of you, the reader, and am hoping you will join me on this journey to pause, breathe deeply, and notice. Being aware of this connection—this embrace of love and hope—takes time and a willingness to pause and notice. But we are here, together, so let us begin with a story.

One day, my daughter and I were baking cookies; she was about seven years old. I had that big KitchenAid bowl ready because we were going to make a double batch and, after carefully measuring out the sugar, she emptied it into the bowl. Now, she was standing up on a stool to see into the bowl, and she was a bit of a distance away from the bowl when she dropped in the sugar. When the sugar hit the empty bowl, the sugar twirled around the mixer and clouds of sweet crystals danced back up into the air. My first instinct was frustration; however, the sun was coming through the window just right, and you could see the sugar swirl and hang in the sunlight. It was beautiful. I paused and breathed and just allowed myself to be stunned by the beauty of the swirls dancing in the light. At that moment, when we were both captivated by the sight, my daughter leaned forward and licked the air. My mind flooded with the words from Psalm 34, "taste and see the goodness of the Lord." So, I leaned in to taste the air too, and we both giggled. The sweetness of that moment has lingered with me for years now. It is a story I retell and reflect on often, swirling it around to see it from different angles and in new light.

PAUSING TO NOTICE

On first glance, that story of my daughter and I baking cookies may seem sweet, or it may seem a bit messy (trust me, it was both!), but it may not strike you first and foremost as a story about God. The effort to reflect on a story, to trace the movements and the way our heart beats in that moment, is a way of catching a glimpse of God's movements. This is like breathing deeply. We normally do not pay any attention to our breathing, but when we pay attention, we can slow our breathing down, which in turn slows our heartbeat down and allows us a different experience of attentiveness. When I reflect on that moment and baking with my daughter, I can see traces of God; I see it in the confidence of my daughter as she learned new skills in baking, in the delight in the beauty of the swirling sugar and crystalized sunlight, and in the patience to pause in the midst of the potential mess and observe from a new perspective. Confidence, delight, patience, perspective—each of these qualities are ones we regularly attribute to God in the abstract. We might even be able to draw a scripture story that shows God delighting in the world or exhibiting patience, but that is still very much in the abstract—it is someone else's story of God. The invitation to be reflective is to see God and His qualities swirling in the light around our physical realities in moments of our own stories, too.

National Geographic photographer Dewitt Jones talks about his photography in a similar way. He has a popular Ted talk titled "Celebrate What's Right with the World." In the talk, he notes when he goes out for a photo shoot that if his attitude is simply one of "we'll see if the perfect shot is there," as if there is a limit to the good photographs and the perfect angles he might find, then he will probably miss it. But if he believes in the limitlessness of beauty and abundance, he will find hundreds of perfect shots. He laughs and says, "mother nature never said, 'There is one great photograph hidden here, only one photographer will find it,' No! Nature says 'bring it on! . . . I'll fill it up with beauty and possibility beyond your wildest imaginings. Right down to my tiniest seed.'" Trusting that what you are looking for is all around you, as near as your breathing, is the type of awareness of God that we strive for as believers. If we believe it, we will see God everywhere. I invite you to slow your pace down enough to allow yourself to take note.

Slowing the Pace

What are the ways you are reminded to slow down and think about God? Think for a moment. Do you have a cross on your wall or a rosary in your nightstand drawer? Is your office shelf full of little icons or sculptures that set a tone for prayer? These are some of the items people have used as intentional reminders to pray. However, psychologists use the term *habituation* to explain the reality that over time, we notice those stimuli less and less. After even as little as a couple of weeks, we no longer notice the pictures hanging on our walls. If we are hoping that the cross on the wall will draw our attention and invite us to pause and pray, we may need to move it every couple of weeks, so we enable ourselves to notice it again.

What about the smell of balsam or the taste of dry red wine—do they remind you of God? Or does the sound of church bells ringing in the distance call you to reflect or pray? Maybe you are reminded of God by a phrase your mother always said; I can remember being a child sitting around our dinner table, and whenever one of us would push away from the table and say, "I'm stuffed!" my mother would smile and say, "What a blessing!" Her reminder to be grateful has lingered with me my whole life. What are some of the cultural practices that you learned from your own parents or grandparents that help remind you to pause and consider God's presence or our connection to something bigger? Were you taught by a grandmother to say a prayer anytime an ambulance passed by, or how the symbol of a Sankofa bird is a reminder to draw from the wisdom of the past to move into the future? A couple of my students from India noted that, as children, they were taught to give a glass of water to any guest who entered the house as a way of learning God's hospitality and care. What are other experiences in your wider community that are shared understandings of when it is appropriate to pause and pray? Such examples are little reminders to pay attention to.

These are experiences that engage our physical senses. We hear or see something and have been taught to associate that physical experience with a reminder to be in tune to a spiritual place. We may hear a bell, or smell the balsam oil, or taste the sugar swirling in front of us that engages our senses and invites us to experience something deeper than simply a taste or smell. The stuff of our everyday life—such as the tangible things we hear or smell—invite us to experience a sense of God's nearness, remind us to slow down and ponder the mystery around us every day. As people of faith, the invitation is to trust that God is as near as our own breath. So if we trust that God is near, then we need to remind ourselves to slow down enough to notice. It may seem odd to start a book about theological reflection by reminding people that God is as near as our own breath. But it is an important presupposition to establish as we think about reflection. We reflect in order to notice our own movement and God's invitation. We reflect theologically in order to allow this awareness of God to shape our identities as ministers and as persons of faith.

Catching our Breath

An important starting point is to pause and breathe deeply. Doing this invites us to remember, in the ebb and flow of our daily routines, to slow our pace down and to notice God. This is a critical skill in ministry and one we probably have already begun to build into our prayer routines and nightly examines. Stopping at the end of the day or starting a day in prayer and reflection helps us to gain a prayerful perspective that will sustain us in our day-to-day lives. Paying attention and knowing when we need to stop and catch our breath in the middle of the day's activities is a slightly different skill that is also important to develop.

As a campus minister I learned that although I lived on campus, I needed at least a half hour to "commute" the 3-minute walk to my office. Inevitably, on most days during this commute I would bump into a student or staff member who needed to talk. But their request was always subtle. They would never simply say, "Do you have a minute to talk?" Rather, as we passed, I would smile and say the usual, "How are you doing today?" and their response, whether in tone or body language, would make me catch my breath. If I paid attention to the physical response, more than their words, I could pick up on their deeper request and would pause and open the door of conversation a little more. I came to learn to trust my read of the other's tone and body language, but I also came to trust my own heartbeat and breath. Inevitably, the change in my heart rate clued me in to the unspoken longing in the person I encountered on each morning commute.

Recognizing our body's cues and paying attention to our experiences of wellness or health limitations are both entry points for rich reflection. Our physical health, as well as the health of the communities within which we live and work, has an impact on our ability to be receptive to the movements of the Spirit in real time. Sometimes our body gives us the first reminder to catch our breath. Physical realities—such as shortened breath, rapid heart rate, or flushing of the cheeks—give us tangible reminders to slow down and pay attention. We have to remain attentive to these clues lest we become too drained to be of any use to those around us. It takes time and energy to be present to the needs of our family or the needs of the community within which we minister. These contexts are both abundant with grace and yet also taxing on time and energy.

As people of faith we know that carving out the space to catch our own breath is critical. It builds a habit of reflection that sustains us in moments of crisis. Physical health is often last on the radar screen. We look at "self-care" as taking time away from the other things on our "to-do" lists. But we need to allow ourselves to pay attention before it becomes a bigger issue. Unfortunately, unless there is a planned need, such as a pregnancy or a crisis such as a life-threatening diagnosis for ourselves or a loved one, we might not pay too much attention to our personal physical clues. Just as the preflight instructions on an airplane direct you to put your own oxygen mask on first before attempting to put the mask on the child sitting next to you, knowing when to catch your breath, and taking the time to do so, makes you more effective in helping others. By catching your breath, you are carving out the space to sit in God's presence and building the muscle memory and the habit to do it more regularly with ease.

In addition to the real need to slow down and catch our breath as part of our self-care, this type of paying attention is also an entry point into noticing God in the midst of life. Paying attention to our physical health allows for reflection on issues of aging and its accompanying limitations; exercise routines or positive self-care can lead to reflections on strength, vitality, and courage; vulnerability in our health might lead to reflections on compassion and suffering and healing. The ability to focus our attention not only on our own health, but on the issues we deal with when faced with limitations in regards to health can provide fertile ground for reflection and noticing God's movement in our lives.

Our relationship relative to the ecosystem that surrounds us is another area where we may need to stop and catch our breath. This ecosystem could be our family, a community of faith, a civic community where we live, the world community or the earth itself. We can run through our day paying little attention to the needs of the community around us or our interconnectedness with it. We might pay attention if there is a specific event or issue that has been brought to our attention, but for the most part, the patterns of living and working do not naturally leave space to ask deeper questions about our context and personal role in the wider picture. These moments of paying attention to the ecosystem around us have to be intentionally built into our routines. We might find the time to carve out a half hour for a 3-minute morning commute, but for some of the deeper questions we need to take sustained time in conversation with others. When we stop and ask questions about systemic injustice, environmental concerns, or do social analysis on the needs of the community in which we live, we are able to imagine ways of responding with our lives that add meaning to the very work we do. Seeing our work as collaborating with God's work in the world is an important by-product of stepping away from our "to-do" lists in order to ask deeper questions about the world and our place in it. We will talk more in later chapters about how the questions we ask form the reflection we engage in, but for now let us acknowledge that slowing down enough to catch our breath gives us opportunities to notice or trace the movement of God. We notice God in our lives and the lives of those around us, and this awareness helps us start to ask the deeper questions of meaning. As Dewitt Jones notes in his Ted talk, "Every day, we get to choose what lens we see the world with." Reflection is about changing our lens.

Paying Attention to Feelings

Patricia O'Connell Killen and John deBeer in their book *The Art of Theological Reflection* speak of the need to pay attention to our feelings as a way to understand the "heart of the matter" of what is happening in any given situation. This is an important tool in their method of theological reflection, and it helps people sift through the various sources for reflection and hone in on the critical moments for focused reflection. They note that our feelings can point the way to what might need further reflection. When we notice anger or love, compassion or frustration rising in ourselves, these are opportunities to pause and notice what might be going on and how we might need to respond. When we come to the end of the day and realize that a particular conversation or incident is still bubbling under the surface of our minds, this is one of the ways our feelings guide us to what moments need further reflection and attention. Killen and de Beer note, "Feelings are the gift of embodied but unarticulated wisdom" (1994, 30). Theological reflection, then, is the task of letting these feelings—and the heart of the matter that they point to—articulate the wisdom inherent there, so that the new truths that emerge can be put into play in life.

Glimpsing God

Health care, feelings, to-do lists, baking with children . . . these are all the basic "stuff" of everyday life. That is one of the most important realizations when pausing to notice God in the world. We are pausing to notice God in the stuff of this world: in the mundane just as in the truly magnificent, in the brief encounters, and in the life-changing events. This has long been one way of theologizing in the Latinx community with *lo cotidiano*—the sacredness of everyday life (Imperatori-Lee 2018, 12). God is there as close as our breath, inviting us to catch our breath, breathe deeply, and look around. Catching a glimpse of God means paying attention to the little details of life. Beginning to pause, to notice, and to pay attention are critical first steps to becoming a reflective practitioner—someone who builds a habit of reflection that impacts how they live, minister, and flourish.

FORMING A SACRAMENTAL WORLDVIEW

Defining Sacramental

The Catholic Church celebrates seven sacraments that call to mind God's presence. These are the official sacraments of the church and, as the catechism teaches, they are a "visible sign to an invisible grace." They focus attention on the moments where God is present in the big moments of life and remind us that God is present in all moments of life. These official sacraments encourage what we call a sacramental worldview that recognizes that every moment can be an unofficial sacrament or moment of Grace. We'll start out by looking at the official sacraments in general and then more specifically at the sacrament of baptism. Finally, we will explore what it means to have a sacramental worldview and how this sacramental imagination is fostered through awareness and reflection.

Baptism, Eucharist, and Confirmation are considered the sacraments of initiation. Each is designed to encourage believers, in different ways, to enter deeper into a relationship with God and with the community of faith. The sacraments of Reconciliation and Anointing of the Sick are the sacraments of healing. They are the sacraments that acknowledge vulnerability either in mistakes made or the vulnerability of physical health or mortality. They encourage us to understand that moments of vulnerability are moments for mercy and forgiveness, opportunities to pull us even closer to God. Dick Westley in his book *Good Things Happen: Experiencing Community in Small Groups* states that we cannot begin to form true community until the members allow themselves to be vulnerable with each other. "Good things happen whenever people gather, but remarkable, even miraculous, things happen when those people share their personal stories and trust enough to reveal their brokenness" (1992, 12). In our vulnerability we are able to recognize that we need one another and that we need God too. These sacraments of healing also teach us how to reconcile with others and how to reach out and care for one another in times of need. The final official sacraments in the Catholic Church are Marriage and Holy Orders. These are both sacraments of vocation and commitment. They point to the ultimate giving of yourself in commitment and service to another person and to a wider community of the people of God.

The official sacraments teach us through their liturgical celebrations how to become conscious of God's presence. These celebrations are very earthly in their design, and that is intentional. Each sacrament has pieces in the ritual that engage the senses. This is because we are human—we experience everything through our senses. We are taught through the ritual of a sacrament that we can encounter God through our senses.

We'll take a look at the sacrament of Baptism as an example. Have you been part of a baptism recently? What were some of the things you experienced in that liturgy? Let's start with seeing—what did you *see* that had meaning? The one being baptized usually wears a white garment. A candle is lit from the Paschal candle. Both of those things are physical images that speak of new life in Christ and the responsibility we have to shine Christ's light into the world. We *hear* the scripture and songs, but we also sometimes hear the sound of running water. One of the earliest writings we have that describes the baptismal ritual of the early Christian community is the "Didache," which scholars agree was written sometime in the first to early second century. It says you should baptize in "living water" (which we take to mean running water like in a stream or river). "But if you have no running water, baptize in other water; and if you cannot in cold, then in warm" (Quasten and Lumpe 1948, 19). Clearly the early church wanted running water, the soothing or crashing sound is an important part of our sensory understanding of baptism. This is tied to the deeper meaning of God's voice like a rushing river of justice in Amos 5:24 or like a gentle voice of peace in Isaiah 66:12, "For thus says the Lord, 'Behold, I extend peace to her like a river, And the glory of the nations like an overflowing stream.'"

Water is something we might *touch* too; the person being baptized feels the water as it is poured over their head. But others touch it as they enter the church and bless themselves. Other ways that we *feel* the sacraments through our sense of touch is through blessings, such as with the sign of the cross that loved ones place on top of the newly baptized head. These gestures and rituals are all different ways the family and community express God's love through touch. When we think of taste, the community gathered tastes the Eucharist. In the early church the sacrament of Eucharist followed immediately after Baptism, and Tertullian notes that they also gave the newly baptized milk and honey. This mimicked what they fed newborns so that the first taste of life in God's family was comforting and sweet. Although we do not do that today, many of our baptisms are followed by celebrations with family and friends involving an abundance of food that signals the abundance of God's love when we gather as a community.

We even have stuff to *smell* in Baptism. The baptized person is anointed with chrism oil, which is a mixture of balsam and olive oils. My husband loves the smell of chrism. He would ask the priest to slather that on our babies' heads, and they smelled of that sweet chrism oil for weeks. Whenever I smell it, I think of their greased-over little heads, knowing they were anointed like precious royalty—a child of God. Even my husband's request at each child's baptism to pour the chrism oil on with abundance is part of the sacrament's intention. There should not be anything skimpy about the abundance of being welcomed into, anointed, and blessed as a part of God's family! The intentionality of building experiences for all of the senses into the sacramental liturgies teaches that God is not off in some far-away heaven, but that God is able to be felt and experienced here in the tangible stuff of life.

These seven sacraments point out that God is present in our lives—that in the big moments, such as when someone is born, or gets married, or is sick, these are times the community gathers around to celebrate or support one another. The sacraments are designed to help us recognize that these are times God is easily perceived in our midst. We are taught too that we can encounter God in the mundane and vibrant moments of daily life by paying attention to what we see, hear, feel, taste, and touch. In moments of reflection, it is often helpful to consider how a particular sacrament is mirrored or echoed in the movements of the moment. Thus, the story of baking with my daughter can bring up thoughts of baptism as similar to her learning or being "initiated" into baking, or Eucharist and communal sharing in the desire to share the cookies. The weaving of our own stories into the narrative of our faith is an important by-product of a sacramental imagination.

But the sacraments also play another important role: they remind us that although these are big moments, God is also present to us in little moments too. This is what is called a "sacramental worldview" or "sacramental imagination," which sees that God is present in every moment in history—every moment. A sacramental imagination trusts that God is here now while you are reading this book, when you are at home with your family, and when you are in awe of nature. Even when we are not necessarily conscious of God's presence, God is there.

Theologian Richard P. McBrien explains this in his book, *Catholocism*: "A sacramental perspective is one that 'sees' the divine in the human, the infinite in the finite, the spiritual in the material, the transcendent in the immanent, the eternal in the historical. For Catholicism, therefore, all reality is sacred" (1994, 9–10). This trust that God is present in the simple moments of our day is what having a sacramental imagination means. He goes on to state, "The Catholic sacramental vision 'sees' God in all things; other people, communities, movements, events, places, objects, the environment, the world at large, the whole cosmos. . . . Indeed, for Catholicism it is only in and through these material realities that we can encounter the invisible God" (1994, 10). McBrien is confirming that a sacramental imagination is the critical tool that helps us to encounter God in material reality. Through our senses we can trace the imprint of God's grace in our lives.

One day my 10-year-old son, Josh, took a picture of a butterfly on a lilac bush in our backyard. That night when I was tucking him into bed he told me, "When I imagine zooming in on that picture, I can keep zooming and zooming in and you know what?! I see God's fingerprints!" I love that image of him zooming in until the orange and black of the butterfly have completely blended with the purple and green of the lilac bush and what he sees is the trace of mystery. Josh allowed his faith to fill in the spaces of experience and notice the fingerprints. You have probably had the experience in life or in ministry where you were talking with someone and you realized that there was far more wisdom in your shared conversation than you would have initially expected. This awareness in the midst of the conversation and trust in the Spirit's presence allowed the conversation to unfold in meaningful directions. This, too, is an example of tracing God's fingerprints between the lines of our words.

Just think for a moment: When was the last time you felt like you were in touch with God's presence in your life? When did a moment seem so full of grace that you knew God was a part of it? Was it when your son or daughter was born? Or when you and your friend worked through a really tough argument and came out laughing? When someone in your church came to talk about a concern and you knew that God was guiding your conversation? When you were surrounded by a vibrant pink and purple sunset? The sound of the breeze? Put your finger on a moment—big or little. That is a sacrament, that is God breaking through with a sense of joy or wonder or compassion. St. Augustine at one time believed there were at least 230 sacraments. He was naming so many moments that the church had to finally decide on a distinction between official sacraments and unofficial sacraments and sacramentals. But when we stop and pause, think through those moments in life, St. Augustine was coming from a place that makes sense: a lot of little moments overflow with Grace.

We see this symbolism in physical realities in other areas as well: the Stations of the Cross move us around the church or the city depending on where they take place, the rosary beads that we touch in our hands guide us through the decades, the flickering candles or the fragrant incense remind us of our prayer rising to God. Each faith tradition has its own physical realities that point to the sacred presence as part of their rituals. All of these are designed to get us to use our senses to imagine God within our hearts. Theologian Anthony J. Godzieba talks about sacraments in his article, "Catholic Sacramental Imagination and the Access/Excess of Grace." He points out that sacraments are, "not a thing to be defined or a text to be decoded, but rather a performance to be experienced, a praxis demanding our participation" (*New Theology Review*, 2008, 16). We have to understand that our sense of a sacrament, or our sense of the sacred in the midst of a moment, comes through using our senses. We have an experience of life that requires us to take an active part in the noticing and naming of God in our midst. Knowing God is not something we do by reading a book or studying theology; encountering God comes from our active participation in our lives with hearts open to the experience of Grace. The "visible sign of an invisible reality" is using our senses to pay attention, to ponder, and to respond within our lives.

Defining Imagination

Another way to look at this might be to take a look at defining imagination. What comes to mind when you consider how you define imagination? If your first thought is of imagination as creating something in your mind that doesn't really exist, then it might contrast or work against our understanding of sacramental imagination as a way of perceiving God's presence in the world. But, if we take a look at the official *Merriam-Webster* definition, we are invited to think more broadly. Imagination is defined as "the act or power of forming a mental image of something not present to the senses or never before wholly perceived in reality." If our imagination invites us to form "a mental image of something not present to the senses or never wholly perceived" then our sacramental imagination invites us to form an image of God not as a static image, but as a reality that we can perceive, even if only partially, through the experiences of our everyday lives. Sacramental imagination invites us to pause, breathe, pay attention, and to notice God's movements in and through our lived experiences. Just as Dewitt Jones notes, "change your lens . . . and you will see beauty and possibility everywhere." A sacramental imagination invites us to see with new lenses or to see with eyes that can see.

Often in our scriptures we hear something along the lines of "Let those who have ears, let them hear" (Luke 8:8) or "Do you have eyes, but fail to see?" (Mark 8:18). These admonitions on the part of Jesus call us to begin seeing the world with sacramental eyes or experiencing the world through sacramental senses. Not only does this invite us to perceive God's presence everywhere, but the admonition to see with eyes that can see or hear with ears that can hear is also an admonition to perceive things the way God might perceive them. This might also be an invitation to change our lens in order to recognize the brokenness or needs of the world and choose to imagine another way to respond, one that brings hope or Good News. Jesus is essentially inviting us to see things from a new perspective, one that can imagine the "otherwise." Godzieba argues that "religion's crucial role in contemporary society is to recognize and actively disclose the 'otherness' that is the sacred" (21). Sacramental imagination defines the way we perceive reality and the way we imagine, hope, and work toward a response of faith that gives the world around us a reason to imagine the sacred as well. We began by trying to be aware of God in the midst of our everyday. Now that we are aware of God's nearness, we must ask ourselves, "What does that mean? What are we being invited to do differently or imagine 'otherwise' in our lives and in the world around us?"

To be sure, we do not need to have a sacramental imagination. Many people can experience life without framing their perspective in light of faith. Deep values of love and companionship and mercy animate people's lives without them considering the presence of God. But if we are a people of faith, and if we are a people who accept that God is not far away in heaven nor distant from our lives, then we are a people who choose to imagine the sacramental grace breaking through in the midst of everyday life. And this sacramental imagination takes work, intentionality, and practice. It takes building patterns of pausing and reflecting that form a habit of seeing and experiencing God in the world.

IMAGINING A WAY FORWARD

In this chapter we wrestle with the notion of noticing God in the midst of our lives and later we will wrestle with the question of how we might respond if we can trace God's movement. But let's start out with the first part: what work and practice does it take to notice God in the first place?

Hardwired to Notice God

An initial way to think about having "ears that can hear" and "eyes that can see" is to look at how we see and hear with our hearts. What tugs at your heart? What inspires you to grab your camera? Stop for a second and take out your cell phone. Take a look at any of the last pictures that you took. What do you see? Is there a picture of someone you love, or is it a funny picture of your pet? Did you snap a picture of something beautiful in nature, or a delicate array of food? I believe we are hardwired to notice God—my son Josh taught me that with his image of the butterfly on the lilac bush. We notice something and take a picture, but do we take the time to zoom in to see God's fingerprints? We grab our cameras to capture pictures of joy or laughter or abundance or beauty. These are images of God, and we snap them up and post or share them without really reflecting on why we noticed them in the first place and how they capture God's movement in our lives. Take a look at your picture again. How do you see God in that picture? What's the "otherwise" you see there? Do you see joy or beauty or love or abundance? Maybe you see pain or sorrow, but your presence there to take the picture shows companionship too. These are all ways that God is breaking through and present in our lives.

Another way of realizing that we are hardwired to notice God is to pay attention to how we go about our ministry. As a person of faith and as someone dedicated to ministry, you are likely to have multiple moments throughout each day where you realize that you are a part of a mystery that is bigger than your vision. Your ability to pay attention to the nonverbal communication of the person who has stopped in to talk, or to put aside your own to-do list to respond to a crisis brewing in the community, are moments where your skill as a minister points to an awareness of collaborating in a bigger vision—an acknowledgment that God is present.

Our hope is to have this sacramental worldview, this imagination that forms our disposition and affirms that God is there. Then, when we look and find the traces of God's movement, we share it with others. Go ahead and share your stories and pictures on social media but invite others to see how these pictures shed light on the sacred at work in daily-lived experiences.

Once we have begun to recognize the sacredness of our experiences, we will get better and quicker at reflecting in the moment. When you are able to catch yourself up in the moment and pay attention to the movement of the Spirit in the conversation, or as you grab the camera, you are more adept at recognizing what you are trying to capture in the photo. You know now that it is more than just the right angle on your mother's wrinkled fingers you were trying to capture, but a glimpse of God in the hands that held yours through life. When this happens, then you are living with eyes that can see. Older people and young children are often more naturally in tune to this type of perspective. My children will often catch a glimpse of my mother with moistened eyes at a family gathering. She is simply soaking in the activity swirling around her and it has moved her to tears: not only tears of joy and love, but also tears of loss and pain. There is deep wisdom in her ability to hold all of that emotion in tension and see it as Grace. Inevitably, one of my kids will lean in and whisper to me, "Noni has her sacramental eyes today." Their recognition of her wisdom is a sweet reminder that they, too, have begun to have a sacramental perspective, and their grandmother is the one teaching them to pay attention. Once we have begun to see with these eyes—once we have started to gain the perspective that sacredness and mystery can easily swirl with sugar and light—we can explore some of our other daily-lived experiences and mine them for the deep sacredness they have as well.

God's Invitation to Imagine and Hope

Merriam-Webster offers a second set of definitions for the word *imagination*: "creative ability" and "ability to confront and deal with a problem." This speaks to the active function imagination plays in providing a sense of hope that things can be more than what they seem. Godzieba talks about poetic imagination in this same way. "The poetic imagination . . . judges the status quo, the 'business as usual' situation of the present as inadequate, not fulfilling enough to match our desires, indeed not humanizing enough. By thinking otherwise . . . the poetic imagination reactivates historical consciousness and allows for the new, the unprecedented, the different, the unprepared-for to break into our consciousness" (19). This notion of imagination takes the present moment and recognizes that there could be something more; there could be something deeper to experience here. A simple example is the sugar swirling in the sunlight when my daughter and I were baking. The status quo response might have been to notice the mess and respond with frustration. The "unprepared-for" response or the something more is to lean in and taste, to notice the layered meanings of confidence, sweetness, and perspective that we can taste in the air. But Godzieba also refers to poetic imagination as activating a response that is, perhaps, unexpected but surprisingly hopeful for those on the margins. An example might be the congregation that notices the status quo of racial injustice in their civic community and imagines a way they can disrupt the injustice with a protest or their presence of support. Together they imagine a way forward that allows the "otherwise" to break into the consciousness of the wider community.

Godzieba says of the Catholic sacramental imagination, "It is the way of envisioning reality through eyes of faith that recognizes that the finite can indeed mediate the infinite, that all aspects of created being can manifest grace . . . the crucial claim is that material 'stuff' has the potential to be a channel of grace" (16). He also talks about the active role we, as believers, have to play in this understanding. It is important to remember that via the sacraments God makes the first move to reveal His self to us or to break into the everyday with Grace. But we can only participate in the sacrament, or in sacramental imagination, if we believe that we will in fact recognize and respond to God.

Imagining an "Other" Way

The active verbs in the definition, "the power of forming an image" or "the ability to confront" imply that we have a responsibility to make the connections between what we experience with the senses and how we perceive God's presence within them. Dewitt Jones states, "belief impacts reality," pointing to the same concept that our perception is impacted by our beliefs. What becomes important to realize is that Catholic sacramental imagination does not stop at simply paying attention to or noticing God. We are being asked to believe in a new way forward, a transformation. "With this imagination, the community probes its immediate situation for new possibilities of existence in the light of God's relationship with humankind and the cosmos" (Godzieba, 21). Our sacramental imagination requires us to do the probing, the confronting, the imagining. It requires us to enter into the experience with a new perspective and to wrestle with what that new perspective demands of us. If we can perceive the world with sacramental imagination, then we are exposing ourselves to the ability to notice the sacred in the everyday, recognize the nearness of God in our midst, and implicate ourselves with the challenge to imagine what that nearness means. If we truly believe that God is as near as our breath—what might we do differently? If we truly believe that the "other" in our community is also an expression of God's image, how might we treat them differently? Having a sacramental perspective invites us to imagine another way of being, another way of living as part of a community. Just as we can trace God in the pictures we take of nature and our loved ones, we are also challenged to consider if we notice God in the images of protestors taking a knee. We will explore these questions more in the third chapter, but here we recognize that theological reflection moves us to some type of response. Noticing the sacred in our midst, attuning ourselves to what that nearness asks of us, and building the capacity to respond is at the heart of why we do theological reflection.

We have begun in this chapter to take a look at some of the moments, stories, and experiences of our daily lives to determine if there is something deeper there, something between the lines of our own stories. This something more, something deeper, invites us to recognize God and discern how we might begin to respond with our lives. So if we have begun to recognize that there is something deeper there, and we have a willingness to spend some time reflecting on what it all means, the next step is to carve out the space to reflect. This "carving out the space" is at the heart of chapter 2.

Chapter 2

Cultivating the Heart

Carving Out the Space for Reflective Practice

One snowy Chicago morning, my children stayed in their pajamas. We had awoken to drifts of snow and calls from school, and the day unfolded for us in a leisurely way as suddenly no one had anywhere to go. About midmorning, as my children were playing on the floor in one of the bedrooms, my oldest son asked, "Mom, what do you do at work?" I had worked late the night before to lead a theological reflection group for deacon candidates, and his question was in reference to my having missed dinner. Rather than try to explain theological reflection to a 10-year-old, I said, "What if I show you?"

My kids loved the idea and gathered around. I placed my big easel paper on the floor between us and asked a few questions like "What is a snow day?" Or "What happens in a city when there is a snow day?" Eventually I got to asking, "What stories from the Bible remind you of a snow day?" and "How do we see God in these types of pauses?" We had a beautiful conversation about our snow day. And eventually we made comparisons between us huddled together in an upstairs bedroom talking about a snow day to the disciples waiting in the upper room and Mary sitting at Jesus' feet. By the end, the children wrote on the easel pad their conclusion: "God gives us days of rest not just so we can have the day off, but so we can sit with God."

What struck me as I watched that conversation with my children unfold were three thoughts: first, children have insights to offer in theological reflection; it is not limited to theologians or even just adults. Theological reflection is important work for everyone. Second, carving out the space to be reflective needs to happen with or without drifts of snow blocking the door. It did not take us too long to unfold that conversation, yet I realized that so many of our conversations are simple or at surface level; we could just as easily carve out an intentional space that brings us into deeper waters more regularly. And finally, the gentle rhythm of the conversation flowed because of our relaxed and comfortable relationships. The warmth of hospitality in community builds trust that creates space for the Holy Spirit to guide or challenge our reflections. That morning with my children took place years ago, before I started my doctoral work, yet those convictions have framed much of the foundation of my thinking on theological reflection. Moments like that helped me to understand theological reflection as a lived experience that engages the stuff of our everyday lives and puts it into conversation with the wisdom of a sacred tradition and the surrounding context in order to seek out the Grace and the invitation of the moment.

In this chapter we will explore theological reflection from several different angles. First, I will begin by defining theological reflection and briefly explore a variety of styles and methods commonly used in the US context. The bulk of this chapter will then focus on building the capacity for reflection in four areas. We'll look at why we reflect, how we carve out the space and time for reflection, consider what in life might be the subject of our reflection, and how we begin our reflections. I hope this chapter helps to reframe theological reflection as an important work for everyone and opens up a myriad of ways to tap theological reflection as a tool for wisdom in ministry and in life.

EXPLORING A LITTLE HISTORY

Defining Theological Reflection

Start by thinking through what you know right now about theological reflection. How would you define it? Is your definition based on what you have read so far in this book? Do you have experiences with one or more methods? What have been the positive outcomes of times you have spent in reflection? What has gotten in the way? What makes reflection theological?

The definition I draw on throughout this book is one I developed over time in researching numerous methods and working with countless groups of students and ministers (and at times my own children) in theological reflection seminars. I define theological reflection as: "Theological reflection at its best is a communal effort to discern God's presence in the world, to carve the space for that presence to invite us into a new vision, and to lay the groundwork for that new vision to take root in how we live our lives."[1] What stands out to you as you read this definition? What resonates with your own definition? What makes you curious to learn more?

Each piece of this definition will be more fully explored throughout this book, and you probably already note the first chapter's focus on discerning God's presence in the world. The presupposition that God is present in the stuff of everyday, which in turn encourages reflection intent on helping us to trace God's movements, is a critical piece of the definition. The questions of theological reflection as a communal effort and the task of carving out the space that opens us up to a new vision are the focus of this chapter. The next two chapters will dig into the invitation to the new vision and how we might lay the groundwork for it in our lives. But first, one additional thought on three words in the definition.

The use of the words "at its best" is an intentional recognition that theological reflection happens in multiple settings and with various nuances, and we do not have to expect perfection. Our reflective practice is not always profoundly transformative, but I believe certain techniques foster reflection "at its best." As we wind through this chapter, you'll note many different ways to reflect theologically on life, but theological reflection as a communal effort opens up the conversation to more depth and wider perspectives than we would encounter if we were to reflect alone. We will talk about this more in the section on *reflecting as dialogue*.

Also, theological reflection does not always happen "at its best" due to issues of facilitation or of failing to build a sacred space for the trust necessary to lay us open to transformation. When we discuss clarifying our goals or refining our hearts for hospitality, we will begin to note the skills that help keep theological reflection focused. Hopefully, throughout this chapter you will gain the skills that increase the odds, so to speak, on theological reflection done well. As we define theological reflection, taking a look at how others have "done" theological reflection might be helpful. Let's explore briefly some of the styles and methods in order to highlight how theological reflection can be adapted for various contexts.

A Brief Look at Method

One of the first known "methods" of theological reflection used to help people of faith actively engage social justice was developed by Joseph Cardinal Cardijin of Belgium, who pioneered the method that has been commonly called "see-judge-act." In 1961 he offered this method of reflection to Saint John XXIII as a guide for preparing Catholic Social Teaching documents. He, in turn, suggested it as part of *Mater et Magistra* as a pedagogy for educators to help students put social principles into practice (para. 236). Cardijin's see-judge-act mirrors the rough outline for many theological reflection methods. *See* suggests taking a look at our experience: to *see* what is happening around us. *Judge* is to put that experience into conversation with the Church tradition: to place a *judgment* on the experience in light of the Church's teachings to determine what is just or right. *Act* is to discern how we might *act* to improve the situation in the future based on this correlation between our experience and the sacred tradition. Although later methods have developed a better sense of the authority of experience, as I will explain later in this chapter, the see-judge-act pattern was influential as other methods took shape.

Robert Kinast, in his book *What are They Saying About Theological Reflection*, speaks of the common methodological form theological reflection has taken, similar to Cardijin's, namely, "It begins with the lived experience of those doing the reflection; it correlates this experience with the sources of the Christian tradition; and it draws out practical implications for Christian living" (2000, 1). He then goes on to describe five distinct styles of theological reflection that have surfaced. His categories are a helpful starting point when looking at the various methods and styles that are commonly used in the US context. The first style he describes is *ministerial style*, which seeks to assist ministers as they work with the problems and issues that arise in their ministerial settings. This style has been employed most often in training programs for ministry, and students often utilize this method as they reflect on their field education experiences. The most well-known example of the *ministerial style* is James and Evelyn Whitehead's *Method in Ministry: Theological Reflection and Christian Ministry*, which they first wrote in 1980 while working at Notre Dame University with divinity students. Their hope was to design a method of theological reflection that encouraged future ministers to consider multiple voices of wisdom as they discerned how they might respond to particular ministerial issues.

The second style Kinast highlights is the *spiritual wisdom* style. Here he draws on Edward Farley when defining spiritual wisdom as: "the wisdom proper to the life of the believer" (Kinast 2000, 16). This style draws on daily experiences of life and looks for the wisdom and the Grace available in even the most mundane moment. The *spiritual wisdom* style of theological reflection is not focused on our responses to issues or concerns encountered in ministry, but rather intentionally attempts to glean wisdom from the daily encounter with God. Patricia O'Connell Killen and John de Beer's book *The Art of Theological Reflection* is an example of this method. We briefly touched on their work in the first chapter when discussing the role of feelings in identifying the "heart of the matter" in reflection. Their work encourages any person of faith to explore how reflection can transform us: "We reflect theologically because it changes us. It allows us to perceive and act differently in our daily lives" (Killen and de Beer 1994, 68).

Kinast identifies his third style as the feminist style. I include here Womanist and Mujerista theologizing as well and see them all as theological reflection through the *liberative lens of women*. Theological reflection through the *liberative lens of women* offers a critique of the pieces of the tradition and context that have played a role in creating barriers and systems of oppression, but it also offers a perspective that includes liberation for all of humanity and the earth itself. This reinterpretation is done with the goal of dismantling unnecessary walls between any person and God's loving embrace. Theological reflection done through the *liberative lens of women* has at its core a critical consciousness about what needs to be transformed in order for all to participate in the Good News. This includes a willingness to transform not only individual experience but the context and the tradition as well. Although there is no single defined method of theological reflection through the *liberative lens of women* per se, theologians such as Elisabeth Schüssler Fiorenza; Elizabeth Johnson, CSJ; Barbara Reid, OP; Deloris Williams; Stephanie Buckhanon Crowder; and Ada Maria Isasi-Diaz, among others, are all women who have engaged sustained theological reflection with a liberative lens in their work. As familiarity with theological reflection increased beyond the 1980s and 1990s, so did the understanding that adaptation was not only possible but necessary. Nailing down an exact method with goals, steps, and sources for each style was no longer as critical as understanding how to adapt the common methods to each particular need and context. Barbara Reid, OP, is the general editor of the forthcoming 60-volume set of the *Wisdom Commentary* published by Liturgical Press. This is an example of extended theological reflection done through the *liberative lens of women* as it seeks to gather a diversity of voices to collaborate on presenting a resource that envisions "God's vision of dignity, equality, and justice for all" (litpress.org).

The fourth style Kinast names is the *inculturation style*. This method begins with a focus on the cultural context of where the theological reflection is taking place and places great authority on the experience within the community. This style is especially critical in missionary settings to show respect and reverence for the communities themselves, and for the need to work against "the universalizing tendency of established theologies" (Kinast 2000, 41). The critical work of this style is to encourage communities of believers to construct the faith that makes sense to them in their context. Fr. Robert Schrieter and his book *Constructing Local Theologies* as well as José M. de Mesa's *Why Theology is Never Far from Home* are both examples of this style of theological reflection.

Practical is the final style of theological reflection that Kinast describes. *Practical* theological reflection has effecting practical change as its goal. It is also a style of theological reflection that focuses on change within the larger society rather than simply within an individual or small-faith community. The pastoral spiral which is featured in the work of Joe Holland and Peter Henriot, S. J., as well as Maria Cimperman, RSCJ are examples of this type of theological reflection paired with social analysis that fosters systemic changes. Social analysis rooted in asking the right questions and exploring right relationships is an important contribution to the understanding of the *practical style* of theological reflection. Questions such as "What does power have to do with this story?" or "How does economics play a role in these decisions?" give a level of depth to reflection that allows for honest exploration of issues of justice with the goal of structural change.

In addition to these five styles, I add Foley's recent *Reflective Believing* as a sixth style. *Reflective Believing* engages theological reflection across religious traditions (Foley 2015). This is especially critical in working with various faith traditions or with folks who claim no faith tradition at all. Foley does an excellent job in highlighting the types of discussions that encourage participants to share their values and develop their skills as reflective practitioners beyond the language of any one particular faith tradition. People who work in religiously diverse settings. such as a hospital, will find that this style offers new ways to enter into reflective conversations.

Kinast's taxonomy of styles of theological reflection offers a workable framework for separating out the field and looking a little closer at various methods of theological reflection. It is important to highlight some of the styles of theological reflection here because they each have their own goals, and, as we consider capacity building for theological reflection, the various styles offer insights from their own focus.

Four areas for building our capacity for theological reflection are important to consider. First, what are the reasons we reflect, and why is clarifying those reasons important to keeping the reflection on track? Second, what are the steps necessary for carving out the space and time for reflection? This includes logistical steps to preparing for reflection by addressing questions such as "On what do we reflect?" and "How do we begin?" Third, how do we refine a heart for hospitality? Skills such as listening attentively, suspending judgment, and knowing our own contextual lenses are offered as ways this can be done. Finally, theological reflection is a dialogue; we'll consider the role of community, sources, and partners we turn to in this dialogue, as well as hone the practice of asking what voices are missing from the conversation.

IDENTIFYING WHY WE REFLECT

Pause for a moment and consider what is important about building a habit of reflection in life. How would reflecting on God's presence and movement in your life impact the way you live or the way you do ministry? What other goals might you have for reflecting? What are some of the skills or resources you need to gain in order to build a habit of reflection?

Thus far we have looked at the notion of sacramental imagination and the belief that we can discern God's presence in the midst of our daily lives. We have also begun to define theological reflection, and have looked at some of the various methods we might draw from as we adapt our own reflective practice. All of this has helped provide us with a framework for exploring the goals of theological reflection and reasons for why this is an important tool for ministry and living a life of faith.

Although the primary goal of theological reflection in the context of faith is to discern God's presence and to explore what that nearness means in the way we live and act, different methods add other goals based on the context and needs of those reflecting. Foley notes almost forty different reasons to reflect (2015, 64) which illustrates the reality that there are almost as many reasons why someone would reflect as there are types of groups gathering for reflection. Thus, being attuned to these goals and willing to adapt as needed are critical skills for reflective practice. In this section we will explore some of these additional goals. Theological reflection builds our resiliency, and it offers an evaluative lens to how we might do things differently in the future. Reflection done within a wider community challenges the narratives that shape our lives and can effect change in social structures. Finally, theological reflection and the awareness of God's nearness causes us to ponder the changes necessary within ourselves to participate in shining Christ's Good News into the world.

Reflection Builds Resiliency

When we have a habit of reflective practice, of pausing in the moment to think about how we might respond or gathering with others to consider what is needed to open a way forward, then we build resiliency that helps navigate life. This is akin to the spiritual wisdom style of theological reflection, which longs to help people draw from the wisdom of their faith as they grow in their relationships with themselves, God, and others. Matthew Bloom in his report "Research Insights" from the Flourishing in Ministry Project (2017) states "resiliency is our capacity to adapt, change and respond to life." He proposes the three important self-regulatory capacities: self-awareness, self-reflectivity, and self-control. Each of these are essential to the process of theological reflection. Self-awareness allows for a critical assessment of our own feelings, thoughts, and actions as well as the lenses that shape our way of being in the world. Self-reflectivity offers the reflective lens to consider the ways our actions impact the world around us, and self-control is the capacity to respond to that information and "distinguish when we should try to change the world and when we should change ourselves" (Bloom 2019, 20). The common serenity prayer, which asks for "the wisdom to know the difference," comes to mind as we consider the goal of resiliency in theological reflection.

An Evaluative Lens

In addition to resiliency, another objective of reflection is to cultivate an evaluative lens on ourselves or our ministry. Often, we are not fully aware of the patterns we follow regularly or the methods of our own ministry. Stepping back and taking a look at the routines of our day or the ways we respond to others is an important goal of reflecting. This type of reflection improves the way we respond in the future and is similar to what the Whiteheads offer in their *Method in Ministry*. When a hospital chaplain takes note of her routine, reflection helps her notice her own blind spots. Perhaps she is conscious of her intentional routine—how she arrives each morning and spends 15 minutes in prayer in the chapel and then picks up the list of patients to visit. She makes sure to pause before each door to enter in a prayerful stance. But reflection through an evaluative lens allows her to notice the unintentional patterns in her routine. Although she is quite intentional about taking on a prayerful stance for each patient, through reflection, she realizes that she was not pausing long enough to say more than a hello to the medical or housecleaning staff that she passed nearly every day. In examining her own movements she was able to realize a blind spot and adjust her routine in order to be present to staff in the hospital as well as the patients. This is a significant recalling of her role as a chaplain to the whole hospital, not just the patients, and can lead to relationship building in new ways.

The goal of reflection with an evaluative lens is also a critical tool when used to unpack those moments where we feel that the way we handled an encounter was not the best. When we step back from a situation and recognize how our own stress levels, or the lingering argument with a spouse the night before, impacted our overly frustrated response to a student, we allow the evaluative lens to guide our reflection. Reexamining the experience in dialogue with others and in light of our sacred tradition as well as psychology or the social sciences can offer new perspectives. Both of these are examples of the ministerial method of theological reflection where we reflect in order to improve how we minister.

The desire to learn from our experiences and imagine a way to better accompany our family or community is not limited to people in ministry. We do this regularly in casual ways. Colleagues reflect together as they bounce ideas around or ask questions that cultivate different responses in their work. Neighbors who gather to consider the needs of their neighborhood school are practicing reflective dialogue. These are all examples of how reflection encourages an evaluative lens.

Effecting Social Change

We might look to the style of practical theological reflection for additional reasons for why we reflect. Reflection focused on creating social change expands beyond individuals reflecting on their own actions to communities of people reflecting together on ways to effect change in their community or the wider world. This happens regularly in our civic society and in our congregational life, but we do not often think of this type of change analysis as moments of theological reflection. When we engage in planning and research proper responses, these are the initial steps of reflective analysis. It becomes theological reflection when we take time to ask where our faith inspires change.

One example of this type of reflection is the parish community that had to consider how to respond to one of the graduates from their grade school. It had been over twenty years since he was a student, but more recently they would find him drunk and asleep on the bench outside the school. Initially the pastor responded on his own by helping him into recovery programs and attempting to support his family through their moments of crisis. But as time went on and the cycle continued the pastor turned to the community, and together began to ask deeper questions about alcoholism and how it impacts their community. They began to explore what counseling services were available in the surrounding town, what other resources were offered for alcoholics and their families, what services were provided for homelessness, and what gaps existed in this support network. They also asked questions, such as how did the economics of the area play a role in the existing safety networks and what were their responsibilities as a congregation. They formulated a response as a community, not only for this one person but also for others in need and for the community as a whole. *Praxis theological reflection*, with its goal of effecting social change, is a critical tool for this type of extended reflective conversation.

Challenging the Narratives

Another way to consider the impact or goals of theological reflection is to consider how reflection challenges the very narratives that shape not only society but the church and ourselves. The *liberative lens of women* offers the perspective that challenging the narratives that have shaped our lives will effect change on a number of levels. Sometimes this happens in subtle ways. Growing up in the 1970s and 1980s, I was not necessarily in tune to the narratives around gender and women that permeated church and society and shaped who I was at the time. The women who fought for and achieved changes in our social structures shifted the narratives of women in countless ways. In the current political climate in the United States, it is easy to forget how much the narratives have changed, even as we know there is still so much work yet to do. Not long ago, I watched a movie with my daughters that I hadn't seen in years, but that I used to love. The excess of offensive and derogatory images of women and violence that I had barely noticed when I was young shocked me. When I saw them again through the eyes of my daughters, I realized how far we have come. The narratives have changed, and although I did not realize the way they permeated my thinking as a child, I am grateful that my daughters can question and challenge the old narratives and continue to move the conversation forward.

Reflective practice leads to faith in a relationship with the wider world or a "public" faith. As Thomas Groome notes, what he terms a "public" faith approach is one that educates people for "a faith that is socially and politically responsible rather than focused exclusively on sacral concerns" (Groome 1991, 150). The task of challenging the narratives is to call our church or our society to look again at its deeper calling in the world. For Groome, the method of shared Christian praxis encourages an understanding of the faith that is also political. "Nothing is more politically significant than shaping the ultimate myths of meaning and ethic by which people shape their lives" (Groom 1991, 12). The capacity for reflective practice builds on skills for active participation in transforming the narratives that shape the world. When we reflect with others, we build a competence for thinking broadly about transforming the structures and narratives that marginalize. Positive and transforming narratives shape positive and transforming societies and cycles for growth that offer Good News. One example of this type of political reshaping of the narratives is to consider the contributions of persons with disabilities into the wider discussion in a church community. Initial conversations around ADA compliance and making sure persons with physical disabilities feel welcomed and are able to access the worship space is a good start. But the hope is for this to lead to deeper conversations around the narratives that shape these decisions. If the narrative is one that focuses on disabilities as hurdles to overcome and the scripture passages we draw from are Jesus' healing miracles, we send a message that persons with disabilities are not whole or complete. But when we consider the narratives that speak of each person formed in God's image or knit in our mother's womb, then we begin to value the contribution that persons with disabilities can offer the community. Realizing that we have made room through the doors and into the pews is one thing, but creating ADA compliance all the way up to our ambo and altar so that they can contribute as ministers and leaders of the community reshapes the narrative into Good News.

Regardless of the method, the most critical goal of theological reflection is to attune ourselves to the movement of God in the world. Focusing on additional goals and considering the types of effects we would like to see helps to provide clarity throughout the process. Keeping our "eyes on the prize" is a phrase that offers insights on how to facilitate and move theological reflection and not get lost in the process. Having a clear sense of the type of reflection you are engaging in with an eye to discerning God's movements will cultivate transformative spaces.

When we stop to notice that we have prayerfully focused on patients but barely said hello to the nurses, or when a community of faith begins to offer meeting space to AA and AL-ANON groups and share access to a psychologist with other local congregations, these are moments where we can trace the way God has moved and moved us to change. We trace the way we have grown in resiliency and critical evaluation to change not only ourselves, but also to create changes in society and in our tradition. Theological reflection has the ability to produce Good News for those on the margins. When that happens, it has shaped and reshaped our understanding of God, our reading of the scriptures, and our participation in the narratives that shape our lives. Theological reflection "at its best" with these goals in mind has the capacity to be profoundly transformative. But cultivating the heart for theological reflection takes more than keeping our eyes on our goals.

CARVING OUT THE SPACE

The second part of the definition of theological reflection states "to carve the space for that presence to invite us into a new vision. " Let's take a look at what that means. Carving out the space can happen in four different ways: carving out the time, considering what we reflect upon, when do we reflect, and how do we begin reflecting. Exploration of the answers to these questions will provide acumen to beginning the process of reflection.

Taking Time

By now you have a growing curiosity about theological reflection and the skills of reflective practice, and you are willing to try to carve out some time and space to see what impact it might have on your life and ministry. Ministers and those teaching ministry students constantly encourage those with whom they work to carve out the space for prayer, reflection, and self-care. As much as we know time away from the mix of everyday concerns is critical, we also have full schedules and busy lives wherein carving out the space for this type of time is hard. Socrates' famous line, "The unexamined life is not worth living" resonates with the practical theologian. If we do not take the time to reflect on and pray about the "stuff" of our lives, then it is as if we have not fully lived.

Anne Lemott, in her book *Bird by Bird: Some Instructions on Writing and Life* notes that good writers train their brain to be creative at a certain time each day. "This is how you train your unconscious to kick in for you creatively" (Lemott 1994, 6). She suggests that you sit down in the same place at the same time every day to write. Long before I had read this advice, I kept a nightly journal. Each night before I went to bed I would jot down some thoughts of what I had done that day or a poem that had reverberated through my head which would pour itself upon my pages. I did this from the time I was ten years old, for about twenty years, until my first child was born. After that, the demands on my time changed drastically and I only sporadically found the time or energy to journal. But to this day, most nights before bed my mind is flooded with phrases I want to remember, or lines from poems yet to be written. Lemott was right: when you train your brain at a certain time each day, you will see creativity showing up on time.

The same is true for reflective practice. When you take the time to regularly gather with colleagues or friends to reflect on the moments in your life, you will recognize that you are in fact becoming more reflective in how you respond to situations on the spot. There is a shift that takes place in your regular responses when your habitus for reflection has been established. St. Ignatius Loyola's Daily Examen is an example of a daily reflection technique designed to cultivate the soul for noticing God's love and mercy. It also includes an honest consideration of faults or areas for growth. Theological reflection can involve this type of examination but also includes contextual analysis that invites action. One student coined the phrase, "missed Grace" after he brought to the table a reflection on his ministry. After the whole discussion unfolded and our classroom chalkboard was filled with scripture passages, saints, and sacraments that touched on the experience and contextual frames to his story, he paused and said, "There's a lot of missed Grace here." He was acknowledging how much the group had unpacked that he had not even considered in the moment it happened and probably would have missed completely if he hadn't opened it up for reflection.

One of the biggest hurdles to carving out the space for reflection is making the time. Many people are already in bi-vocational work and stretched thin, balancing their ministries or their work alongside their family or community needs. Good people are always busy doing good things, and making the time for reflection can feel counter intuitive. But theological reflection builds the critical skill of perspective that is necessary in navigating ministry and life. Another helpful image Lamott offers her students is when you sit down to write, think of it as having a one-inch picture frame to look through as you try to determine your focus for writing. Reflection is much the same way. If you turn your thoughts to even the smallest details of life, you begin to reflect on those details regularly and notice an improved perspective in the midst of life. You will begin to notice the way sugar swirls in the sunlight, the way your heart rate speeds up when someone says "Hello," or the wrinkles of age and laughter on the face of one of your elderly parishioners. A group of friends or family that gathers in conversation encourages accountability and commitment. Groups of psychologists or psychiatrists, cohorts of hospital chaplains, and curriculum development teams of teachers are all professional groups that gather at regular times to plan, debrief, encourage and imagine together. Theological reflection for people of faith offers the same type of support and accountability.

It begins with deciding you will give it a try, deciding that you have missed too many moments of Grace and you would rather not miss any more. Begin by first making the time to reflect on your own. Later we will talk about gathering with others to reflect. But start by carving out 5 minutes of time to use your one-inch picture frame and notice where you see God in the details.

On What Do We Reflect?

Once you have decided to carve out the time and space for theological reflection, you may find yourself asking, "On what do we reflect?" Here is where experience takes center stage. We start by looking at the stories of life. One suggestion is to unpack an experience or a story that lingers with you. Perhaps you feel you did not do something well, and you would like to gain the perspective that comes from reflecting with others in the Spirit. Or you may realize that an incident keeps resurfacing in your mind, and you recognize there is still depth that has yet to be discovered.

Some of my students get caught up on what exactly to call the "story": is it a ministry incident, an encounter, a moment, as if calling it a "story" makes it feel too childish. I encourage them to not get too hung up on what to call it, or what makes a good story for reflection. If we have a sacramental imagination that trusts God is present throughout life, then any moment in life can be cultivated through reflection. Years ago on National Public Radio they had a segment in their popular show "Wait Wait . . . Don't Tell Me!" where they would throw a dart at a map of the United States. Wherever the dart landed they would then proceed to randomly call people in that town to learn about the town and the people who called it home. That became my favorite metaphor for theological reflection. If we believe that God is present throughout our lives, then we could "throw a dart," so to speak, at any moment in life and be able to get to know it a little better and reflect on where we see God's movements there. To be sure, we might not have as deep a reflection as we would on, say, a reflection that starts with more emotional weight. But you might be surprised.

One of my students one time wanted to "test" my theory, and during class he "threw his dart," saying "at 4:30 pm next Tuesday afternoon I'll write what I am doing." He decided he would bring that moment to see if we could reflect on anything of substance. The next week he came to class and reported that at 4:30 pm last Tuesday he was standing in front of his fridge looking for something to eat and realized that there were way too many leftover containers in the fridge. He noted that, apparently, he was one of only a few guys in his religious community who was willing to eat leftovers. This was the story that he brought to the theological reflection table and challenged the notion that we could find anything rich to reflect on with that as our starting point. The conversation meandered through emotions of frustration with community members and thoughts on being frugal and not wasting food, to environmental justice and past experiences with food insecurity, and eventually, we even engaged the theology of a tabernacle and the sacredness of hospitality that dwells within our community and sustains us. Although it started out as conversation about a random moment in time, it led to a deeper reflection about what food and hospitality and Eucharist mean in the context of communal living. This is an example of the *spiritual wisdom* method of theological reflection. When we pause to consider any moment and trust God is guiding us, then anything from leftovers to snow days can become a sacred canvas for theological reflection.

As we begin learning reflective skills and what story to bring for reflection, it helps to remind ourselves to frame a story with a beginning, middle and an end. This is important for a couple of reasons. There can be a temptation to turn theological reflection into a "self-help" session if the story is one that is, as of yet, unfinished. If there is still an argument going on between a pastor and the parish council or if the emotions are still raw after the funeral of a loved one, the group can lose its focus and, rather than open themselves up to the Grace of the story, they can try to become problem solvers and a support system for the storyteller. Stories shaped with an ending allow the whole group to "own" the experience and dig into it for reflection and insights. If we hold onto an incident too tightly or we force someone else's story into our own agenda, we may short circuit the depth of the reflection possible. One older student started out the semester commenting on how she hated theological reflection. She had learned theological reflection years earlier when she was a novice in her religious order, and the facilitator felt it was not a good session unless someone cried. The focus on raw emotion and self-help detracted from the effort to use that emotion to open us up to God's transformative work. Through the course of our time together, this student came to understand the deeper meaning of theological reflection and saw it as an important tool for her future ministry.

Theological reflection is not about our agenda. We share our stories in reflection in order to understand how our story situates us in the wider story of life's meaning. There is a universalizing response to any shared narrative. When we hear someone else's story, we begin to hear pieces that remind us of our own story. Those connections allow us to have a dialogue and challenge each other to notice the meaning and substance present. Groome talks about the effort to see our own stories in the wider Christian story. "People always retain the seeds of the capacity to place their life in dialogue with the Christian story" (Groome 1980, 255). This dialogue between the story of our lives and the wider story of faith or human history is an important piece of theological reflection. When we listen attentively to another's story, we listen for where and when we recognize the wider story of God, or the world and our place in it. Careful not to assume that our familiarity with characteristics of a story mean we understand the point of view or the context of the other, we trust that attentiveness in dialogue helps the reflective process along and increases our ability to notice God's movement and invitation more clearly.

When Do We Reflect?

The habit of reflection is developed over time. We begin with the intentional carving out of time and space to reflect. We may start with reflecting on our own in quiet moments, but we will want to eventually gather a group of others with whom to reflect. Over time that practice affects how we reflect in the midst of life as well. If we have become adept at reflection, then we can notice the questions we ask or the ways we respond in real time. We will find in time that reflection can happen in many different settings. Some ministers find it helpful to reflect right after a ministerial incident has taken place; to take some time and jot down a couple of notes not only to summarize the conversation that just took place, but to identify things they noticed about their own actions or feelings, or to note what they saw in the responses of those they were companioning. This personal reflection gives insights and helps our memory as we bring it to a larger reflective conversation with others.

In addition to personal reflective time, reflecting with a group of colleagues or staff at regular intervals does the heavy lifting for building our capacity for reflection. This is the shared reflection that enhances our ability to gain perspective and notice our own blind spots. In this shared reflective space, the Spirit is able to move and challenge our insights as they form. A regular reflective group is key to building a capacity for reflection that happens in the moment. Chances are you might be sitting in the middle of a congregational planning meeting and the discussion has reached an impasse with no vision for moving forward. You probably would not stop everyone and say, "Let's do theological reflection about this," but you will find yourself asking the right questions to guide the discussion along. Asking the right questions and engaging the various perspectives adds relevancy to theological reflection, and such adept leadership results in productive movement. As hard as it might be to find the time, the enrichment and growth you experience are well worth the time spent.

How Do We Begin?

Theological reflection can have a couple of different starting points. Throughout the ages, the starting point for theological reflection in preparation for homiletics is to start with sacred scriptures. The preacher may start with the Sunday readings from the lectionary, but a good homilist will then reflect on how the stories in those readings are reflected in the stories of the community. Groome suggests a starting point in Church tradition. As an educator, he first considers the theme he would like to teach, such as reconciliation. From the theme he moves his students to consider where reconciliation plays a role in the regular moments of life. Questions, such as "When have you had to say you were sorry to your mother or little brother?" or "When have you felt the joy that comes from an apology accepted?" will prompt his students to further reflection.

Practical theology and the discipline of theological reflection in particular have moved to put experience as the central starting point for theological reflection. Even if we begin with scripture or tradition or context we still come back to how this scripture or tradition is reflected in our own experience. Experience takes center stage. We bring the stories of our lives into creative conversation with the sacred texts and traditions of our faith and also into dialogue with what is happening in the context around us. This is all a type of dialectic that challenges each participant to open up to the insights and perceptions of others around the table. We will talk more about these dialogue partners and sources later in this chapter.

Another interpretation of the question "How do we begin?" might be a question of the logistics of gathering people together. People are busy, and finding the time to forge new relationships with others looking to build their reflective practice skills is not something you do every day. Start by thinking about the wisdom figures you turn to most often; you might look at those you call when you need an opinion or who you seek out for conversation when you need to unpack your day. Try to identify three or four other people—colleagues, friends, and community members—whom you could invite to get together with once a month. Even if they live at a distance, such as classmates or childhood friends, with today's technology you can arrange a regular Zoom or Skype meeting. You do not even need to get everyone to have the same available time if the group is willing to have reflection take place in an email thread. I have designed theological reflection for online students where they do theological reflection in a discussion forum with no synchronized time. Students log in and write responses to each other in defined time periods and within suggested parameters regarding posts and replies. This has been very successful, especially considering that some of our small groups span multiple continents and time zones. Examples of these variations are available in chapter 6.

Once you have a few people willing to give this a try, start with the stories of life, ministry, or of stuff going on in the world. We start with what we see or hear or notice and open it up to see how it can point to an awareness of God. The promise in Matthew 18:20 that "where two or three are gathered in my name, I am in their midst" encourages us to gather together, trusting in God's presence and attuning our hearts to the perspective of shared wisdom.

REFINING A HEART OF HOSPITALITY

Theological reflection invites people into a sacred space of transformation. This type of space is vulnerable and is created by cultivating our hearts and our reflective times to be spaces of hospitality and thoughtful availability. Emma J. Justes speaks of thoughtful availability as not only listening, but also of "listening for what is not being said" (2006, 45). There is a sense of hospitality that comes with the experience of theological reflection in a communal setting; hospitality of the heart willingly opens the door for conversation and growth and movement toward empathy. Hospitality is developed through cultivating the various skills that we will talk about in this section.

In her work in interculturality, Presbyterian minister Claude Marie Barbour speaks of "mission-in-reverse," which is where missionaries "begin their relationship to the people and cultural contexts as a new example of the 'tabula rasa,' without ideas, convictions and talents" (*The Healing Circle*, Bevans et al. 2000, 4). When using this approach the minister takes on a "childlike" dependency, realizing the importance of mentors to help out when they make mistakes and need help identifying prejudices. Children listen with a heart that is willing to learn, ask questions without assumptions, and generally do not hesitate to ask for help with comprehending what they do not understand. That approach to missionary work offers some insights to the practice of theological reflection as well. Through theological reflection, we develop the skill of listening to learn from the other, of attuning our hearts to see how together we can trace the fingerprints of God in our lives. We also learn the skills of suspending judgment, attending to our feelings, paying attention to our contextual lenses, and formulating questions that invite deeper dialogue.

Listening to Learn

Listening is a key skill for any dialogue, including theological reflection. We first listen to what is happening in our life and consider bringing it to reflection. In the midst of reflection, we listen to the stories of one another and we listen for clues to the movement of God in our midst. As we look to put our experience into dialogue with context and tradition, we listen to the narratives of the culture and the context and the voices of the world around us in order to include their perspective in the reflection. We listen to the *sensus fidelium*, the voices of the faithful as they try to live their lives of faith; we listen to the sacred stories of our faith traditions; and we listen gently for the little hints and clues to God's invitation for growth.

We will unpack a lot of these reasons for listening in the section below, but let us begin here with a focus on the basic skills needed to listen to one another in the communal conversation that is theological reflection. Many great books are available that discuss listening skills and, specifically, listening skills for ministry which can cover the topic better than I plan to do here; however, let us take a quick look to understand the role listening to learn plays in theological reflection.

Listening takes intentional effort to stay focused on the other person. Although different studies offer different numbers, there is consensus that the average person can understand somewhere between 450–1,000 words per minute. On the flip side, we can only speak between 150 and 250 words a minute. What that means is that while we are in a conversation, our minds can be distracted. We may listen to what the other is saying, but often we are also thinking about how stiff our chair is or how hungry we are feeling. Sometimes we are focused on trying to enter into the conversation with our own story or question. What someone else is saying jogs a memory of our own or a curiosity, and we can end up distracted by what is going on in our own minds rather than remain focused on staying attentive to the person before us. We hone listening skills by practice: we practice listening to the other's words and their nonverbal communication. And we hone our skills by intentionally paying attention to the other. But beyond simple listening techniques, we also listen to learn from the reflection.

Putting aside our distractions and gently attending to another person opens up a sense of hospitality and empathy. Foley states, "sometimes silence is the most respectful and intelligent choice we can make" (2015, 35). We are creating a sacred space where the other trusts they are heard and we are willing to learn. We might not have answers to their issues or the perfect words to soothe their concerns, but our attentive presence goes a long way to breaking down walls of isolation and division. Listening to another person offers a sense of empowerment or agency too. When we listen to another person, their voice takes center stage and we temper our own need to be heard or right or in control. We learn to listen for the cues of where the Spirit might be guiding a conversation and for the right question or perspective that can offer a sense that the other is heard and their story has value.

At times we might ask a question that stems from skepticism about something someone just said. In these cases, we commandeer the conversation with our own questions or concerns. When this happens, we run the risk of cutting the reflection short and losing perspective. Discerning between questions that offer direction to the reflection and questions that turn the focus in unimportant directions is another way we listen to learn. When we feel distractions interrupting the conversation, we can ask ourselves if the question we want to ask is something that turns the focus to ourselves, or if it is something that can continue to guide the conversation on a reflective path. We must attempt to keep a listening ear and open heart in the midst of theological reflection.

Suspending Judgment

Another way that we unintentionally cut a reflective conversation short is by implying a sense of judgment through our questions or statements. Although we often do not realize it, when we ask a question or make a statement, we ask it with a slant that exposes if we agree with or have a problem with what is being said. This type of judgment leaves the other feeling vulnerable, and they most likely will not risk exposure again. If we are able to suspend our own judgment and engage the other in an honest reflection on what is happening and what are some of the reasons for their actions, we are again carving out a space of listening to learn from the other, which allows our reflection to be open and honest. Although Cardinal Cardijin utilized the word judge in his "see-judge-act" methodology, the effort within theological reflection is not to judge the person, story, or actions against the scripture and tradition, as if to seek out what is right, but to lay our own story alongside the story of our faith tradition to determine what insights they have to offer each other. Suspending judgment is an important component of the liberative lens of women for theological reflection, too. The willingness to look honestly at those pieces of the tradition or context that have been oppressive or painful to various groups offers a hermeneutic of suspicion that does not judge but rather opens the reflective process up to exploring where the Spirit leads. This type of reflective practice allows participants to pay attention to the movement of the Spirit and propose adjustments that breathe life and hope into the tradition once again.

Attending to Feelings

Another area of refining our hearts for hospitality is through paying attention to our feelings. Killen and deBeer place a strong emphasis on being in tune to our feelings. They aver, "Feelings are the gift of embodied but unarticulated wisdom" (30). This method of theological reflection is rooted in the ability to discern our feelings and allow those feelings to point us toward the "heart of the matter" to be explored in reflection. Hospitality toward our feelings and the role they play in our actions is not something we consider often. Feelings like anger or frustration, and even feelings of joy or love, are sometimes ignored or denied. Paying attention to our feelings and discerning if they hold insights for what we value or how we understand a situation is a way of refining our sense of hospitality. If a sacred space has been carved out for theological reflection, then people are more willing to name their feelings and share them in the group. This shared vulnerability brings the whole group to a deeper level of community building. When feelings are shared, participants offer insights and perspectives on how those feelings impact their actions, their reactions, and their attitudes moving forward. As Foley suggests, "The implication seems to be that if you are willing to wager on nurturing a heart tuned to the experiences and needs of others, then a new and unusual path of wisdom opens before you" (2015, 74). Foley, Killen, and deBeer suggest our feelings help point the way to embodied wisdom. Paying attention to our feelings is also an activity of knowing our cultural lenses. Different cultural contexts express and share feelings a very differently, and being able to name our feelings as well as the cultural norms around them brings additional insights.

Knowing Our Own Contextual Lenses

Each of us experiences life through a certain set of cultural and contextual lenses. When we refine a heart of hospitality, we notice the contextual lenses that are operative in us, in those with whom we reflect, and in the context of the situation upon which we reflect. The way that we think, make decisions, or respond in ministry is based on learned behavior that shapes our operative modes of acting in the world. This learned behavior is seen as cultural identity, or the context within which we live. Our contextual lenses are influenced by our physical abilities or our age or our gender; they are shaped by our social or political norms. Our contextual lens is made up of many pieces that shape our identity. As an American Catholic laywoman, married with four young adult children, I come with a completely different set of lenses than my colleague who is a Franciscan brother, or any of my students who were born in different parts of the world or who live by different faith traditions.

This is not to suggest that because we have different lenses we might not understand each other, but to encourage—as Claude Marie Barbour suggests—a willingness to begin by being aware of our own lenses as well as humble recognition of how much we do not know about the context of the other. Also important is the way we examine the theological lenses through which we look as we reflect on God's movement in our lives.

We refer to this as our operative theology. This is the theological framework that shapes the way we operate as people of faith. Theological reflection provides us with an opportunity to reflect critically about how our understanding of God, our knowledge about God, the ways we have learned to encounter God in ritual, in community, and in our religious education impacts the way we encounter God in our lived experience. Theological reflection gives us the tools to ask what type of *ecclesiology* is operative in the way a particular community responds to a particular crisis. This may vary even for communities on different sides of the same city. Through theological reflection we can explore what type of *Christology* or *ethical considerations* we draw from as we engage in a protest march or watch it from the sidelines. Each of us have our own understanding of the Trinity or Eucharist or suffering or reconciliation which is shaped by how we have learned these theological constructs. Understanding these as the theological lenses which are "familiar" to us, but perhaps different for another person in another contextual setting, is also a critical piece of discerning God's presence and invitation to transformation.

Our effort to know our own contextual lenses and to pay attention to the cues of someone else's context lets them know we are thoughtful and focused on them and their story. We learn about their context and learn to draw insights from it for perspective. We also realize that we can pick up on the assumptions or blind spots operative within others or ourselves. Knowing our own lenses and asking contextual questions of others helps us to gain perspective and to learn from them in a spirit of mutual respect and dignity.

Asking the Right Questions

Questions can help unpack the contextual codes and thought processes that shape our actions. Asking the right questions rather than insisting on being right is another way to refine a heart of hospitality. Two people have shaped my reflective practice by introducing me to the simple technique of repeatedly asking a question to generate insights. One of my first graduate courses was on theological reflection with Patricia O'Connell Killen. She invited Fr. Jack Shea to guest lecture in our class for an afternoon. He introduced his favorite simple "method" for theological reflection. He suggested that we could very easily get to the depth of a reflection by simply asking "why." Even now I laugh and think "Any mother of a two-year-old knows this method!" The number of times my toddlers asked "why" never felt so much like theological reflection, but I understood what he was driving at. So, if someone starts out by saying, "I passed a homeless man on my drive to work and I was feeling hopeless because I see so many of these guys each day." We might ask, "Why do you think you pass so many homeless people each day?" or "Why do you feel hopeless when you pass someone who is homeless?"

and whatever they answer, we continue to turn it into a question of "why." If his answer to our question is, "I feel hopeless because giving a dollar or two doesn't really help." We would follow with, "Why doesn't a few dollars help?" And so on. He contended that by thoughtfully asking "why," if you kept going, the trajectory would lead you to ask some profoundly tough questions about homelessness and feelings of hopelessness that may challenge us to consider where we find hope and how we might act to bring hope to others. This method of asking why is also highlighted in Cimperman's text and attributed to Nancy Sylvester, IHM, but I first learned it in that class.

Another simple question is "So what?." My friend and colleague, practical theologian Fr. Edward Foley, can be heard on many occasions earnestly asking, "So what?." Sometimes he responds to someone sharing thoughts on what they are researching theologically or a conversation about committee decisions, but his pointed question digs at the deeper meaning of why would we make a decision or delve into research if it did not have a practical implication in the lives of real people. By simply asking "So what?" we invite the other to tell us more about the importance they place on their actions and challenge ourselves to grasp for the deeper meaning that might cultivate Good News in our own.

Questions of "why" or "so what" are not the only questions that impact the way theological reflection unfolds. Holland and Henriot and later Cimperman positioned the questions we ask as a critical part of their method of social analysis. They ask questions like, "What does power or money have to do with a situation?" or "How is leadership chosen in a particular context?" or "What is the history behind how the situation escalated to this point?" The questions we ask open up reflection that carves out the space for new perspectives and wades into deeper waters of insight and understanding. Naming the types of questions we ask as "clarifying" or "probing" signals where we are in a reflective conversation and the direction we are headed.

When someone shares their story for reflection, we might begin with clarifying questions in order to make sure that we understand their story and are not inferring or filling in the blanks of their story with our own viewpoints. These types of questions are not only designed to clarify a story but also get the person sharing to feel that they are heard and that we value what they have to offer for reflection. Clarifying questions build a sacred space where the group can open the reflection up and consider the various perspectives that come when we trust the process.

After clarifying questions have allowed each person to have a better understanding of the incident, we then begin to ask questions of others—those sitting around the table as well as the sources of tradition, sacred texts, and contextual insights. Here the probing questions or social analysis questions play an important role in attending to the various sources that we might turn to for insights. Probing questions also open the dialogue up to the movement of the Spirit. The practice of asking questions helps us to explore what we might learn from the social sciences, from our sacred texts or traditions, or from our own contextual lenses. The Whiteheads speak of this as "attending" suggesting the importance of not only asking the right questions but entering into a dialogue open to the insights and transformation that is possible through reflection.

REFLECTING AS DIALOGUE

The last set of skills we will talk about in this chapter center around the notion that theological reflection is a dialogue. The questions we ask begin the dialogue process in an effort to lay our lives and our assumptions, our feelings and our responses open to a faith-filled analysis that invites perspective and growth. This dialogue trusts we will find God's perspective when we attune our hearts to our own lenses and tune in to the wisdom and expertise of those around us. Reflection on our own gives one dimension of insights, but reflection with others, either in real-time conversations or over the ages with thinkers and writers from various schools of thought, helps to expand the horizons of perspective. In theological reflection we can have many different dialogue partners. Those we choose to reflect with, those we turn to for insights or listen to learn from impacts of the direction we take. Who we turn to in order to reflect theologically on life says a lot about the type of reflection we long to have. Natalia Imperatori-Lee suggests, "A dialogue among narratives, power relationships are laid bare, marginalized voices can be included, and through dialogue unity can emerge where uniformity was once imposed" (2018, 5). Dialogue that includes the voices of those on the margins expands the way authentic community develops.

Role of Community

Gathering a group together for regular reflection builds a learning community. As we discussed earlier, such groups of people become a community of trusted dialogue partners who offer perspective on the effort to discern God's presence and our response. Just as Matthew 18:20 states, "Where two or three are gathered in my name, there am I," we trust that a group of people reflecting together are shaped and inspired by the Spirit's movements in their midst. I tell students who are practicing facilitating theological reflection to "trust the process and trust the Spirit." The insights and questions of others around the table present an authentic challenge that pushes us deeper to examine our own assumptions and perspectives and encourages us to engage our experience with a willingness to see it from new angles. There have been plenty of times in the midst of facilitating theological reflection where I think that I am not really sure where this will go next, but I find myself trusting the process and am awed by the way the Spirit moves the conversation. A good question raised or the right amount of silence allows the conversation to catch a breath and move deeper. In these moments of conversation I realize that if I had tried to shape or contain the reflection, if I had assumed we had hit the depth of the well, I would have short-circuited the process. Theological reflection unfolding within the context of a community is a Spirit-filled endeavor that takes trust and patience.

Sources to Draw into the Dialogue

In addition to the people that we gather together for reflection, we draw other sources into the dialogue as well. As we have mentioned, our own experience is the first critical source. Reflecting theologically is not practical unless we are willing to explore our own experience and mine it for the wisdom it has for our faith. A preacher who talks of the scriptures, but never draws a connection between the scriptures and the lives of the people in his or her community says very clearly that the experience of the community holds little, if any, importance in their reflecting. The insights that come from putting experience into dialogue with the sacred texts or traditions of our faith is at the heart of contextual theology. José de Mesa speaks of experience and context when he discusses the efforts of the community that reclaims its authority over the colonizing narratives. He discusses the Filipino term, "'*Pagbabalik-loob*,' [which] means—a return (*pagbabalik*) to the most authentic self (*loob*), where the true worth of a person lies. Rather than rupture, the intent of this conversion is to get in touch, to affirm, to connect, to be nourished by the wisdom and genius of the culture" (2003, 70).

Just as important as the source of our experience are the sources of our sacred texts and faith traditions. Exploring our experience in light of the stories and the themes of our sacred texts or traditions affects the reflective dialogue. Groome talks about this as seeing our story in line with "The Christian Story." Any story or incident we bring to the table is an experience that will not only resonate with others at the table in one way or another, but we can probably find traces of the same story in our sacred texts. Drawing from scriptures and traditions in theological reflection helps to shed light on how hundreds of others have found hope or redemption in and through their daily lives. We engage the sources of traditions and sacred texts by reflecting on what from these sources offers insights for how we shape our response to God. Just as the image of a tabernacle revealed insights in a conversation about leftovers in a community fridge, or the Eucharist considered in a reflection on baking cookies, we gain wisdom by allowing our reflective practice to draw multiple sources into the dialogue.

The other sources that are critical to engage in the midst of theological reflection are the contextual sources that can offer insights either contemporary or timeworn. Engaging contextual sources means remaining attentive to the lenses that shape our perspective. Or as de Mesa notes, reclaiming our contextual lens is done when we consider the dynamics that have shaped the narratives of the past or how we might frame the narratives of today (70–71).

Engaging contextual sources also means acknowledging how gender or sexuality, age or ability, race or socioeconomic status frames how we see an experience. Utilizing social analysis questions, we engage the contextual sources for insights that can help us frame the experience and our responses. Drawing from scientific evidence when reflecting on the impact of our church parking lot on the water supply in our community, or asking questions of a psychologist when wrestling with the best way to support someone with an addiction are important ways to draw contextual resources into the dialogue of theological reflection. We not only bring contextual resources in to tap them for the wisdom they might offer to particular situations, but we also engage them as a way to tune in to our own blind spots or growing edges.

An example of engaging our contextual lens is the extended reflection with one student who mentioned, "I don't really offer anything when our family talks about my grandfather's health. I am one of the youngest in my family, and I'm female, so I guess I never thought I had anything to offer." As the group reflected on what she was learning through her practicum as a hospital chaplain and her contextual lenses as a young Latina in a large extended family, she began to appreciate that her growing knowledge of the health care system and its nuanced technical language was a resource her family did not realize she could offer. Discussing ways her age, gender, and cultural context has kept her from seeing herself as a wisdom figure in a time of crisis in her family compelled her to offer her insights more confidently. She later reported that her family was incredibly grateful, not only for the wisdom she shared with them but also for the way she was able to communicate concerns and issues to the medical team. Theological reflection empowered her to notice her blind spots and build her confidence to offer her expertise in her own family as well as at her ministry site.

Considering Authority

When Cardinal Cardijin first introduced the method of see-judge-act, there was a sense that the *judge* portion of the reflection was to take what we have experienced and hold it up to the tradition in such a way as to come to understand the right or true way to respond in light of the tradition. Theological reflection has developed in such a way as to recognize that each source in the dialogue has authority and can reveal God's truths. Placing our experiences in conversation with the scriptures and traditions in light of contextual understanding allows us to tap the wisdom held in each area. When it comes to exploring how we might encounter God in our midst, we trust that all sources reveal something of the nature of God's presence. Theological reflection values the authority in experience just as highly as it values it in the other sources. Thus, the young chaplain who was asked to baptize a child who was stillborn confided that, in the moment, he knew that saying what he has learned—"The church teaches that baptism is for the living"—was neither pastoral nor merciful. Rather than give the "right" and quick answer, he trusted the authority of his experience with these young parents, and gently led them through prayers and blessings that brought solace. He saw the critical issue in that moment was to share God's unwavering love for the child, God's steadfast compassion for them in their pain, and hold the family in a prayer of lament. He knew pastoral compassion in that moment revealed God's presence more fully than could be done through explaining what the Church taught. Building a habit of reflection helps people to respond pastorally in the moments when the "right" or "correct" response falls short. Theological reflection is to wrestle with God's abiding presence in each source in order to respond in ways that are transformative and filled with hope. In addition to valuing the authority of experience, theological reflection allows experience to critique and challenge the other sources, too. However, reflecting from personal experience is not without its blind spots, too.

Paying Attention to Who Is Not at the Table

One of the blind spots that theological reflectors often have is that they neglect to attend to all of the possible sources that should be considered in their reflection. This is often referred to as asking, "Who is *not* at our table?" This question has a couple of different layers. First, it asks whose voice is missing from the present conversation. This could be the result of simply not having the person on hand to take part in the conversation or sometimes intentionally leaving someone out of the conversation because their presence would challenge the status quo too much. A second layer to this question asks what voices of wisdom should be tapped when we turn to the sources for insights. Asking the question of which voices are missing from the reflective process opens us up to considering the insights and perspectives we might otherwise miss.

Let us begin by asking the question of whose voice is not at the table and able to take part in the conversation at hand. Often, someone brings a story to the table and the group will begin exploring by asking questions of motive that are unanswerable. For example, if someone shared a story noting how they were frustrated because the person they tutor in English is regularly missing class. As much as the group may want to focus on the reasons for these absences, unless the tutee is at the table to answer any of the questions being asked, the group cannot assume her answers. Instead of asking clarifying questions that cannot be answered such as "is the distance she needs to travel too taxing" reframe the discussion and focus it back on the person who brought the story forward. Questions along the lines of "Why do her absences make you frustrated?" or "What are some of the ways you have discussed the absences with her?" are more helpful at getting to what is within our control to adjust and adapt. That is a simple example, but we are tempted to allow our own assumptions or inferences shape the way we see a scenario play out, and to render the one not there voiceless in our assumptions. Keeping the reflection focused on perspectives for growth and change within our control is an important practice. In addition, recognizing the voices both at and away from the table of reflection gives those perspectives a chance to offer insights.

A second way to note whose voices are not at the table is when we engage the various sources in our reflection: in the midst of a reflection, we might begin asking what our context or tradition has to say about this incident. This is, as the Whiteheads note, the way we "attend" to various sources. But we need to pay attention that we are not only listening to the voices that "agree" with us or the voices we already know well. It takes intentional digging to ask "Whose voice do we need to hear that we are thus far ignoring?" The source of tradition has opened up this type of reflection rather slowly when it comes to including the voices of experience and science. Climate change is one area where the church values science and has allowed its findings to challenge and impact church teaching; however, in other areas, developments in science have been avoided. Theological reflection that challenges the authority of a source is vulnerable. Thus, how the church has resisted engaging the experience of her people and the voice of science in its reflection and writing on issues concerning the LGBTQ community is one of vulnerability and frustration. More recent reflections including *Male and Female He Created Them: Towards a Path of Dialogue on the Question of Gender Theory in Education* released in 2019 by the Congregation of Catholic Education suggest that the church understands the roles of listening and dialogue play in healing. The voices of LGBTQ Catholics, ignored as part of this conversation for so long, are hoping such listening and dialogue opens up a space for them to be a part of the church they love in their wholeness.

This inclusion of marginalized voices is a critical piece of theological reflection. The practical theologian's affinity with asking "So what?" or "Why," is to insist that reflection leads to Good News for those on the margins. When we ask, "Whose voices are missing from the table?," we lay a foundation for dialogue that values those whose voices are most commonly marginalized. By asking these types of questions, we allow the voices on the margins to begin reshaping and reauthorizing the centers of power, privilege, and the narratives that shape our lives.

Facilitating the Dialogue

Theological reflection is a dialogue; as we can see from the section above, this dialogue has a profound ability to transform our very lives. This dialogue takes humility of heart and honest assessment in order to lay us and our world open to the movements of God. We notice God's fingerprints in the stuff of our everyday lives that we bring to the table for reflection; we trust God's authority is revealed in each of the sources we pull into the conversation, and we hear God's voice in the midst of the dialogue itself. Facilitating theological reflection is a little like Moses noticing the burning bush. We take off our shoes because we know we are on holy ground. We do not get hung up on our own imperfections as participants. But we try to pay attention; we pay attention to the stuff we might not notice, the stuff alive and burning with God's love and compassion all around us. We look with eyes that can see, we notice common things aflame, we step closer with a humble curiosity, and in doing all of this we find ourselves present to God's love in surprising ways. We will talk more about facilitating theological reflection in chapter 4, but the dialogue, the paying attention to, and discernment of God's presence in the world brings us to the next piece of our definition: "to invite us into a new vision." Theological reflection carves out the space to unpack the stuff of everyday life and opens us up to the surprising vision God sets before us. If everything we have said thus far lines up and we believe as Pope Francis suggests, "Our God is a God of surprises," then we have to embark on the next chapter wondering about this new vision and asking Jesus' parabolic question, "Do we have eyes that can see?"

NOTE

1. This definition first appears in my doctorate thesis project in Ministry from the Catholic Theological Union in 2012. The early thinking behind this book and several sections of chapters 3 and 4 originated in that thesis-project.

Chapter 3

The Wisdom of the Parables: Developing Ears that Can Hear and Eyes that Can See

We have a new puppy in our house and new puppies bring chaos. In an effort to stem the chaos a little, we added a baby gate that confines her to the back porch. While this is temporary—just until she is housebroken and abandons her taste for shoes—it is still a hurdle for some in the family. My three-year-old was in the back porch when she had to go to the bathroom. "Mom," she called, "I need you to get me out of jail." After I lifted her into the kitchen, she walked toward the bathroom then turned and said, "You know I'm still in jail—I'm just on the side with the bathroom now."[1]

This story has always felt to me like a modern-day parable: "The Reign of God is like the little girl playing with her puppy." There is something so quaint and commonplace about a puppy and a need to contain the chaos and a three-year-old thinking about gates and bathrooms. And yet each time I reflect on it, it slams me with the twist that demands I open my ears and listen again. My daughter had no idea what she was pointing out in her monologue on justice, but her unconditional love for her puppy and the deep desire in her heart to not be separated from it painted a baby gate as a jail, and no matter what side of the fence you sat on—you were still in jail.

"You know I'm still in jail—I'm just on the side with the bathroom now." In the moments after she said that and skipped off to the bathroom, I was stunned. Flattened. My head and my heart were rearranging to see if I could really ask the question she had just answered. As long as anyone was in jail, were we all in jail? Did I love the "other" deeply enough, miss them and their part in my world profoundly enough to consider myself in jail too—until everyone is free? Do I have ears that could hear that?

DO WE HAVE EARS THAT CAN HEAR?

These questions, "Do we have ears that will hear?" or "eyes that will see?" are provocative statements that frame many of the parables Jesus tells in the synoptic Gospels. These questions and the parables they frame also offer a provocative lens for theological reflection. This chapter advances a couple of presuppositions about parables that are significant as we explore theological reflection. We will begin by listening to the voices of several biblical scholars about the pattern found in parables. Next I will highlight the pattern in parables by exploring the parable of the woman and the yeast from Luke 13:20–21. Amazingly, this two-line parable says so much; we will have fun digging into it together. Third, we will explore what parables tell us about the challenging vision of the reign of God. Finally, we will come back to the question at hand: "Are we willing to have those eyes that will see?" Throughout this chapter I hope to demonstrate that parables offer a provocative lens of justice that is necessary for theological reflection. This awareness moves us to the next chapter to explore parables as a lens for theological reflection.

DO PARABLES HAVE A PATTERN?

Many modern scripture scholars point out that parables follow a pattern. They begin with a familiar scene from everyday life or they have some quality about them that is surprising or shocking and that challenges the listener to see things in new and unexpected ways; they are also open-ended, leaving the listener to figure out what might be the right response. C.H. Dodd offers one of the earliest definitions of parables that point to this threefold pattern. He writes, "At its simplest the parable is a metaphor or simile drawn from nature or common life, arresting the hearer by its vividness or strangeness, and leaving the mind in sufficient doubt about its precise application to tease it into active thought" (Dodd 1961, 5). In these three statements, we can begin to see the pattern of parables: first, they are stories drawn from common life; second, they include something that is vivid or strange, which highlights the third element that "teases" the mind into active thought. He goes on to argue that parables, through their metaphors and their anchoring in the everyday lives of their hearers, bring about a new understanding of what it means to live in the presence of God. For Dodd, the structure of a parable and its ability to draw or "tease" the hearer into glimpsing the message in the life of Christ is critical. "[Jesus] used parables to enforce and illustrate the idea that the Kingdom of God had come upon men [and women] there and then . . . . This world has become the scene of a divine drama . . . it is the hour of decision" (Dodd 1961, 159). The implication of Dodd's statement is that Jesus' parables are providing a glimpse of how God sees the world, and the minds of those listening are "teased" into active thought—wrestling with how they might respond.

Another scripture scholar, John R. Donahue, considers Dodd's definition and lays out four elements of a parable: (a) its poetic and metaphoric quality, (b) its realism, (c) its paradoxical and engaging quality, and (d) its open-ended nature (Donahue 1998, 6). Both authors appreciate the metaphoric quality of parables, noting that the comparison made in the parables is between something familiar and something that is not easily grasped. This harkens back to our discussion of imagination and sacramental imagination discussed in chapter 1.

Parables are simple stories about everyday types of activities—a traveler on a road, a shepherd caring for sheep—and yet, it is in these simple scenes that we can catch a glimpse of God and God's vision for the world. Parables often begin framed with a statement like, "The Kingdom of God is like . . . ," which plays on the metaphor comparing the reign of God to the simple scenes of daily life. Dodd sees this as the world becoming the scene of divine drama. Donahue avers, "What is pointed at by the metaphorical prediction is ultimately beyond the power of language to express . . . it must be experienced" (Donahue 1998, 9). Thus, the parables set the scene for the listeners to recognize, and possibly even experience, the presence of God through the stuff of everyday life.

What Is Familiar?

Donahue notes that Jesus' parables are "stories about ordinary individuals and ordinary events but are told in such a way that people from every age and culture have seen their own life 'replayed' in these short vignettes" (Donahue 1998, 14). The wisdom of the parables is that they take the ordinary experiences of farming or baking and compare them to the extraordinary mystery of God and God's reign. No matter when we hear the parables, they offer a glimpse of how God encounters us in our own day. "The parables claim that the arena in which God summons human beings to the risk of decision is the world of everyday existence, is that same world in which the life of Jesus unfolded in dialogue with the mystery of God" (Donahue 1998, 14). As we noted in the first chapter, God is present in our everyday lives and, as these authors suggest, through parables we wrestle with what that nearness means. As Donahue notes, the "risk of decision" is when we come to terms with the reality of God's nearness, when we see the vision pointed to in the parables, then we have to decide "so what?" Does it matter to us at all?

What Is Surprising?

A common part of the metaphor in many parables is "the reign of God is like . . . ." The second half of the metaphor is a simple scene of daily life;

however, a twist challenges us to see the vision offered. Perhaps the most obvious one is the shepherd who leaves the flock in order to save the lost one. Dodd states that the parable is "drawn from nature or common life, arresting the hearer by its vividness or strangeness"; this is what Donahue refers to as the "paradoxical and engaging quality" of parables. "In terms of image and subject matter, the parables are realistic, but in the unfolding of the parable the realism is shattered" (Donahue 1998, 15). As a listener, when we begin to step into the story presented in the parables, the natural tendency is to pick out the points of similarity between the story and our own. But, as the story progresses, we begin to see an unfolding that is counter to expectations. This strangeness is confusing and challenging.

Drawing on John Dominic Crossan's thinking, Donahue states, "The most fundamental message of Jesus' parables is that things are not as they seem, that you must be open to having your tidy vision of reality shattered" (Donahue 1998, 16). The parables present a vision that is surprising or shocking. Perhaps they make us uncomfortable, but they also offer a challenge. If we listen to a parable with the humility of an open heart willing to be transformed, then in the arresting strangeness, we find a deep thread of hope or truth about God. "People who hear that things are not the way they seem to be may experience what they have not dared to hope . . . *a vision of reality which becomes a presupposition to ethics*" (Donahue 1998, 17). In the shock or surprise of the parables, we can begin to recognize the vision God is inviting us to see, and in turn the expectation to respond. This vision offers a sense of hope or Good News if we dare to see things in this fresh way.

What Is the Invitation?

The third element to the pattern in parables is what Donahue refers to as the "open-ended" nature of parables. Dodd's description is longer and it nuances the open-ended dynamic in subtle ways: not only in that parables leave "the mind in sufficient doubt" but also in that the parable is able to "tease [the mind] into active thought" (Dodd 1961, 5). The surprising or shocking pieces in a parable challenge us to reconsider or question our "tidy vision of the world," which in turn opens the door to contemplation and transformation. The open-ended nature of a parable causes us to question reality and the way things are while also contemplating the meaning of the parables and the way things could be. Donahue discusses how this open-ended dynamic of a parable is conversational in nature. "The parable is a question waiting for an answer, an invitation waiting for a response" (Donahue 1998, 19). Thus, all those who hear the parables throughout time have the same challenge, "Do we recognize the vision of the reign of God presented in the parables?" And if so, how do we respond? Donahue avers, "The parables speak of that change of heart (*metanoia*) which is necessary to respond to the presence of God" (Donahue 1998, 158).

Reid highlights the basic flow or structure of parables as presented by Dodd and points out that "Jesus' parables do not stay at the level of the familiar. Always there is a catch . . . they are startling and confusing, usually having an unexpected twist that leaves the hearers pondering what the story means and what it demands" (Reid 2000, 7). Here we see the conviction that listening to the parables and opening ourselves up to seeing things in a new way invites, or perhaps even demands, that we respond.

Pause for a moment and think about some of your favorite parables. Can you pick out these different elements in them: the familiar scene, the stuff that surprises you, the question waiting for an answer? In order to have a clearer understanding of this flow or pattern of parables, it might be helpful to look in depth at one small parable. The parable of the woman and the yeast in Luke 13:20–21 is only two sentences long, but even in those two lines it says so much. Exploring this parable will give us an opportunity to look specifically at how this parable illustrates key elements of the structure or pattern in parables. We will take a look at the words of the parable as they appear in order to notice how each piece of the parable fits into the threefold pattern.

THE FLOW OF PARABLES DEMONSTRATED THROUGH LUKE 13:20–21

Again he said, "To what shall I compare the Kingdom of God? It is like yeast that a woman took and mixed in with three measures of wheat flour until the whole batch of dough was leavened."[2]

Let us begin with the first line: *To what shall I compare the Kingdom of God?* This introduction to the parable is a common phrase Jesus used to frame a parable, and it sets in motion the parable's metaphoric quality. The metaphoric connection to the reign of God is not simply the yeast or the woman or the flour, but the whole situation. The whole scene gives insights into the reign of God, and looking at the whole scene as an image of the reign of God can lead to transformation. At first glance, this small parable shows a familiar scene. A woman is baking bread.

Yet even in this familiar scene something "surprising or strange" emerges when the pieces are examined. Next the parable states, *it is like yeast*. To Jesus' listeners, yeast might have been a piece that was a shocking. Yeast found in most US supermarkets today comes in tidy little packets that we mix with water to activate. But yeast used by those hearing these words from Jesus was a bit more like today's sourdough starter. Practically speaking, it was a bit of fermenting starter or a piece of old bread from the last loaf that was mixed into the dough to begin the fermentation process. So there is value placed on the yeast and the fermenting that helps the bread to rise. But this is also a surprising piece of the parable, as Reid points out, "In every other instance in Scripture in which leaven occurs, it represents evil or corruption" (Reid 2000, 299). This negative connotation could lead one to conclude that the yeast was something unpleasant; something that no one wanted to admit was in the bread. Unleavened bread was considered holy.

Although Jesus warns against "the leaven of the Pharisees" (such as in Matthew 16:12, Mark 8:15, or Luke 12:1), in this parable the leaven is a necessary part of the reign of God. The yeast might be a reference to those on the margins or those with whom we would not usually associate, yet here the parable is challenging that we need the yeast in order to rise. This challenges our "tidy view of the world." We might not like to admit that those on our margins or those we see as imperfect are a part of our reality as the agents of change. It is just as hard to admit that they (and the change they represent) are needed in God's vision of the reign of God. This parable presents a challenge to see yeast as part of the transformation necessary for the coming of the reign of God. Reid continues, "For those who are privileged, it is a summons to change their attitudes to those they consider 'corrupt' and to see them as the very ones who provide the active ingredient for the growth of the community of God's people" (Reid 2000, 300). This is just the first part of the parable that provides a challenge to our view of the world.

Next the parable says *a woman*. Another paradoxical quality of this parable is the focus on a woman. Even though it is a familiar image to see a woman baking bread, there is a challenge to Jesus' listeners, and even to us today, to recognize that a woman and the basic work of daily bread baking can be part of the reign of God. Here, Jesus asks the listeners to put themselves in the place of a woman baking bread. This parable offers the opportunity to see the world of a woman and her work as a part of the transformation of the world. Reid points out, "Jesus' teaching and practice . . . invites believers to envision God in such a way that women and men are both seen to reflect God's image equally" (p. 303). This would have been a challenge in Jesus' day and, unfortunately, it can still be a challenge today.

So far we have discussed: *To what shall I compare the Kingdom of God? It is like the yeast that a woman . . . took and mixed.* I love the intentionality of the verbs used here. The woman's actions are intentional in their placement of the yeast and in their attention to mixing, kneading, working the yeast in with the wider ingredients. In some translations of the bible the verbs are *took* and *hid*. That sense of hiding the yeast in the process of bread baking helps to frame the thought that yeast was not welcomed. When making bread, one might know that simply putting yeast and flour together does not result in a reaction. The ingredients need water, they need warmth, they need to be worked and kneaded together in two cycles that involve time for resting and rising, and finally shaping. Yeast alone does not transform the batch. It needs the taking and mixing and the patient waiting to get results. Thus, this provides an image of the work and collaboration with God necessary to bring about God's reign. That sense of our daily work as collaboration with God gives validation that the simple chores of life, our work and participation in society, can be part of the Good News in the world.

The parable goes on: *with three measures of wheat flour.* Do you know how much "three measures" of flour is? This image is an additional point of surprise and challenge in this parable. Three measures of wheat flour is roughly the amount of flour needed to bake about 50 loaves of bread. I love baking bread, but even with my daughters on hand to help, we have never tried to undertake the job of kneading 50 loaves of bread at once. However, in this parable, one woman uses a bit of leaven, works it, and kneads it, until the whole batch rises. That is patient, careful, and hard work.

Reid points out that "three measures of flour," can be found three other places in our scriptures (Reid 2000, 303). Sarah uses three measures of flour to quickly put together a meal for Abraham to set before the three visitors in Genesis 18:6; Gideon uses three measures of flour for bread and other gifts to set before the visitor that came to tell him to take up arms against the Midians in Judges 6:19; and Hannah takes three measures of flour with her along with other gifts when she presents Samuel at the temple in 1 Samuel 1:24. "In each of these instances, the large scale baking prepares for an epiphany. So, too, the parable in Luke 13:20–21 portrays the work of a woman as a vehicle for God's revelation" (Reid 2000, 303). In all three stories the encounter with God either promises something that the host saw as impossible, or is a thanksgiving for something thought impossible, and in each of these stories the large sums of flour were used to prepare for an encounter with God. There is an abundant feast being prepared, an abundant response to the gift of God's presence. Those who begin to see the invitation will join in the preparations by opening their hearts to transformation and by collaborating in building the reign of God.

The final line states: *until the whole batch of dough was leavened.* The third piece of the pattern in parables is that parables are open-ended. They do not tell the listener how they should respond, but they invite the listener to consider if they want to participate in the vision offered. The reality is that, although the parables are open-ended, they demand some type of a response—even no action is a type of response. The parables invite those who hear them today to cultivate a receptive heart willing to hear the Good News, to receive the blessing and be transformed by the presence of God in the world.

In this parable, the open-ended nature comes in the very act of rising. Yeast and flour alone do not make the bread rise, God's actions of kneading, warming, patiently working, and waiting transforms the whole batch. Both yeast and flour need to be changed by their proximity to one another, by the possibilities the other provides. The open-ended nature in this parable shows Jesus asking his listeners and those of us who read the parable today to ponder the same question: "Will we participate in the rising?" The whole process is the patient unfolding of God's vision. Luke Timothy Johnson points out that this parable follows closely after the moment where Jesus heals the woman in the synagogue on the Sabbath. He states, "Luke puts [this parable] within a highly charged situation of conflict. And he does so deliberately . . . in just such small and hidden acts of liberation as he has worked in the synagogue are the victory over Satan's Kingdom being won" (Johnson 1999, 214). The invitation in this parable is to consider if we will engage in these small hidden acts of transformation, if we are willing to be mixed in along with those we "other" and if we see this as the Good News of salvation.

This exploration shows how a simple parable invites a complex array of interpretations that offer a vision of what it means to live in the presence of God. The pattern that draws a metaphoric line between the day-to-day stories of life and God's vision challenges the hearers with a twist to their comfortable understanding and leaves open a question as to how one might respond is evident in even these few sentences. Let's take a quick look again at how much is packed into this two-sentence parable:

> Again he said, "To what shall I compare the Kingdom of God? It is like yeast that a woman took and mixed in with three measures of wheat flour until the whole batch of dough was leavened."

Can you see the familiar scene? The woman baking bread, her arms elbow deep in a bowl of flour, yeast, and a little water—kneading the dough. Can you see the surprising elements: the woman as a representative of God's transformative work? The abundance of flour spilled out all over the scene anticipating the abundance of God's reign? Can you sense the challenge inherent in the yeast having a central role; are you challenged to admit we need those on the margins of society as much as they need us if we are to build the reign of God together? And look closely. Can you see God kneading us (or perhaps *needing* us) to participate in the rising? Just pause for a moment and consider that. This whole scene invites us to consider if we are willing to rise, if we are willing to collaborate in God's abundant Good News in the world. Are we willing to be *needed*?

All of the parables have these qualities. They carve out a sacred space by carving out a familiar scene, and then in that familiar space they offer a twist that surprises or challenges us, that makes us wrestle with a new vision. Then they leave us there to ponder how we are called to respond. Think of some of your favorite parables again. Open them up and take a look. Spend a little time reading them. Can you see the pattern a little more clearly now?

SO WHAT? WHY TELL PARABLES?

Perhaps the question "so what" comes to mind as we look at the simple parable of the woman and the yeast. Why would it matter to explore parables or even life through the lens of this threefold pattern? I find myself answering that question by exploring another question entirely: Who tells such stories and why? Crossan takes a couple of steps back from the words of the parables themselves to look at Jesus, the teller of parables. Crossan sees Jesus as telling parables that get his listeners to step into the world he has created in order for them to be able to see more clearly the world that needs changing. He is suggesting that the parables were Jesus' way of critiquing the established norms of society and pointing to a new way of acting in the world. Crossan grounds his thinking in "the thesis is that Jesus is proclaiming what might be termed *permanent eschatology*, the permanent presence of God as the one who challenges world and shatters its complacency repeatedly" (Crossan 1992, 26). The parables are Jesus' way of getting us to begin using our sacramental imagination. They invite us to recognize God's permanent presence in our midst.

Reid also takes a look at Jesus and the invitation in the parables he told. "While multiple interpretations are possible, the preacher always tells the story slant, inviting the hearers to take a particular position in the narrative . . . and the stance to which [Jesus] invites his hearers is with the marginal" (Reid 2000, 9). What both of these authors are pointing out is the presupposition that parables bring Good News for those on the margins. William Herzog pushes even further by stating, "The parables were part of that larger strategy, which included a prophetic critique of the systems of oppression and of the ruling class and proposals for prophetic action" (Herzog 1994, 264). Each of these authors is encouraging us to consider the vision that Jesus is trying to open up for his listeners. His repeated statements along the lines of "let those who have ears let them hear" challenge his listeners to see things the way he sees them, to pay attention to the way God can be revealed, and to open up to the transforming vision presented.

WHO ELSE TELLS PARABLES?

Theologian Edward Schillebeeckx also explores the notion of parable and, more critically, Jesus as the parable God tells the world. In *God Among Us: The Gospel Proclaimed*, he offers a series of homilies that provide a pastoral approach to his theology. In the chapter "Jesus' Story of God," he discusses at length his understanding of Jesus as God's Parable. He does not, however, simply try to define what a parable is, but instead begins by saying, "The telling of a parable . . . is a remarkable phenomenon" (Schillebeeckx 1983, 28). He then acknowledges the storyteller and the act of telling a parable. Schillebeeckx's starting point is not the internal dynamics of the parable form, but rather the dynamic of conversation between the storyteller and the listener.

For Schillebeeckx, not only must parables be interpreted, but it is also critical to understand who tells them, since that provides the key to their ultimate and appropriate understanding. If we can understand who is telling us the story, we have a better chance of understanding why they are telling it to us. So how does Schillebeeckx understand Jesus as the parable God tells humanity? When reflecting on the shock factor implicit in parables, Schillebeeckx looks to the actions, messages, and life of Jesus in the Gospels, primarily the Gospel of Mark. As an example, he points to Mark 2:1–3:5, where in quick succession Mark threads together five actions of Jesus that force others to formulate an attitude about him. Schillebeeckx states, "Not many people understand the story that Jesus himself represents . . . but the parable is so provocative as to make a neutral attitude towards it impossible" (Schillebeeckx 1983, 30). Jesus' actions of healing, forgiveness, and celebration all paint a picture of someone who was so paradoxical to the conventions of his time that the responses to him were anything but neutral. People either loved him or were shocked by him, and one response was to crucify him. But, yet, that was also the shocking piece of the parable of Jesus. For even those who were open to the parable of Jesus' life, those willing to be uncomfortable and challenged by his critique of the established norms, were comfortable enough in Jesus' story that they too were shocked by its twist. Jesus' life was paradoxical to some: Jesus' death was paradoxical to others and Jesus' resurrection was paradoxical to all. "People have to make up their minds, because the story of Jesus does not just disclose a new and different possibility of living but subjects our own, actual, much-cherished attitudes to devastating criticism" (Schillebeeckx 1983, 30).

ARE WE WILLING TO ENTER INTO THE DIALOGUE?

When looking at how Schillebeeckx might understand the flow or pattern in parables, we can begin with how he might frame the familiar.

Schillebeeckx's lens is that a parable "forces us to look at our own lives" (1983, 28–29). This is analogous to the thinking of both Dodd and Donahue who suggest that a parable draws upon the familiar experiences and, through that entry point, shocks the listener into a new vision and response. The point of the parable is to get the listeners to struggle with the complacency of accepting this world as it is. Jesus juxtaposes himself to the realities of ordinary experiences of suffering—of injustice, of marginalization, of erasure, of denigration—and in that parabolic contrast opens up new ways to counter those realities ourselves. He points to these new ways through how he lived his life by inviting everyone to the table, regardless of whether they are tax collectors, prostitutes, or Pharisees. And he points to them in the stories he tells, such as the parable of the "Lost Lamb" (Luke 15:1–7). Here, Jesus not only points out that the lamb is lost, and God's preference is to stand with the lost, but he also exposes the herd mentality that couldn't care less about the one off alone.

Jesus encourages a critical evaluation by the stories he tells and by the way he lives his life. Schillebeeckx notes this dual approach by saying, "The man spoke almost exclusively about the coming kingdom of God. . . . His actions, life and words were a parable of God; that is, in the life of Jesus it became manifest that his God was a God who is concerned for human beings" (1983, 132). Through the familiar moments of the parables, we can trace God's presence. Through the shocking moments, we are challenged to critique our world with fresh eyes. As Schillebeeckx points out in another book, parables are like "experiences of conversion, crucifying experiences which lead to *metanoia*, lead us to change our mind, our action, our being" (1993, 29).

Crossan also engages this line of thinking when he discusses parables as a dialogue. The fact that there is a storyteller assumes that there is also a listener. He points out that the element of surprise in parables assumes a listener who is someone other than the storyteller. "One can tell oneself stories but not parables . . . it takes two to parable" (Crossan 1988, 69). Herzog also speaks to this point: "[Parables are] not a monologue to be heard and accepted but an invitation to conversation and communal reflection" (1994, 265). Thus, parables are a conversation in which the storyteller carves out the space for their hearers to be simultaneously shocked, hopeful, and free to respond. As Donahue states, "Theologically this means that the parable is a form of discourse that appeals not only to the fascination of the human imagination with metaphor, or to the joyous perception of a surprise or paradox, but to the most basic of human qualities: freedom" (Donahue 1998, 19). What each of these authors is suggesting is that parables, by their very nature, assume a storyteller and a listener. This conversational nature points out that parables are about communication and relationship, seeing things from another's perspective and yet having the freedom to respond.

ARE WE WILLING TO BE PARABLED?

The open-ended invitation and freedom to respond is also present in the parable named Jesus. Schillebeeckx draws on Mark 8:29 and the question Jesus puts to his followers: "Who do you say that I am?" Schillebeeckx encourages the realization that everyone who hears Jesus' story and that question has to answer it on their own. "No one—neither historians nor scholars nor even the first Christians—can answer this question for us. As we hear the parable, we are confronted with the question whether we will stake our lives on it" (Schillebeeckx 1983, 31). Jesus' message, which points to God—and God's love for humanity, God's preference to stand with the lost ones, God's promise that all will rise—calls us to a *metanoia*, a new way of existing that is more about relationship than anything else. When we respond to the open-ended parable of Jesus, the response is more than a profession of faith *about* God, it is a response *to* God: thus it is an acceptance of the offer of relationship.

Our response shows our openness or sensitivity to the critique the parable makes on our life. As Schillebeeckx states, "A parable does not need a speaker to comment on it . . . or an interpretation. The parable itself interprets our life, our existence, our actions" (1983, 30). Robert W. Funk also weighs in on this saying: "Parable as metaphor is designed to retain its own authority . . . the parable is not meant to *be* interpreted but to interpret" (Funk 2006, 43). When we think about the parables Jesus tells, or Jesus as the parable God tells, then we can understand what it means to be interpreted by the parables. By opening ourselves up to the critique of the parables, we are challenged to see ourselves as God sees us. Listening to the parable with ears that can hear, requires a "willingness to be parabled" (Crossan 1988, 39). Are we people that listen to parables and wrestle with their meaning in our lives? As Schillebeeckx and Donahue have pointed out, every age must engage the parable and decide how they will respond. It would seem that Pope Francis agrees. Not only does he agree with the thought that God is surprising us, but he also asks, "Are we a person on a journey?" Are we willing to be moved by the vision God presents in the parables?

Parables tell the promise of a familiar story; they draw the listener in and point out a paradox, which can be a moment of grace, but they are open-ended as well. The listener is always free to respond. Elizabeth Johnson suggests, "Jesus took this good news which he preached in spoken parables and enacted it in living parables" (Johnson 2010, 5). In his own life and actions he sets before us the best example of how to participate in the reign of God. This notion of responding to God in the parable of Jesus helps us to realize that it is not simply a personal change of heart that he is driving toward; it is a sense of relationship and a deep bond with community. God is bent toward humanity, as Schillebeeckx points out, not only to tell us how much we are loved, but also to show us how much we *should* love. Schillebeeckx points out that the question of "who do you say that I am" is not one that calls only for our response to God, but also for our response to the world. "It is a question from 'the world' about the public visibility of our Christian identity . . . Can we Christians still in word and deed, 'give an account of the hope which lives in us'" (Schillebeeckx 1981, 841). Our actions are more than a collection of ethical responses to the needs of those around us; anyone can do that from a secular perspective. For Christians, Jesus, as the parable of God, is the foundation of our hope, and his life is the example of the way to step toward solidarity.

CAN WE WRITE OUR LIVES IN PARABLE?

The question of relationship with God and community also challenges our concept of time. Jesus' message was not just about our relationship with God in the future, but our relationship with God and one another in the present moment as well. "It is plain from the life of Jesus that 'present' and 'future' although distinguished, are essentially bound up together. . . . What is becoming clear already is this: Jesus makes a connection between the coming of God's rule and metanoia, that is, the actual praxis of the kingdom of God" (Schillebeeckx, 1979, 152). Our response to the parable of Jesus throughout history is what makes us a community of Christ's followers. Thus, as Schillebeeckx states, "the church becomes a community in which those who have opened themselves to the critical force of the parable of Jesus' life tell stories round a shared table" (1983, 31).

Schillebeeckx suggests that the Christian response is to tell stories. However, I would argue that the story to tell is not just any story, but a parable. We can tell a parable with our lives. The response to God in parable might mean living a life that is familiar, shocking, and open-ended, inviting all those around to see in this community gathered in solidarity the presence of God. Schillebeeckx talks of writing a fifth Gospel with our lives. "In the end we have here the convergence of two stories, the story of the Gospel tradition of faith and the story of our personal and social life which, in the best instances has itself as it were become 'gospel' a fifth or umpteenth gospel" (1993, 152). Perhaps as we take up Schillebeeckx's challenge to participate in the story of Jesus as a response to God, we might find that we too are challenged to live lives that are parabolic. Earlier we discussed how a parable assumes a storyteller and a listener that are two distinct entities and that parables surprise their listener. If we are now telling the parable, then the way we live our lives should surprise God back.

WHAT DOES PARABLE OFFER THEOLOGICAL REFLECTION?

Parable offers a provocative lens for theological reflection, and how this might look will be discussed in the next chapter. A parable as a lens for theological reflection moves the conversation beyond noticing God in our world, to asking who it is God says that *we* are, and remaining open to the transformation that perhaps can only be reached through solidarity with those furthest from the centers of power and privilege. Theological reflection is an opportunity to build a habit of reflection that opens us up to new perspectives, and the lens of being interpreted by the parable of God offers a provocative path forward. If what Elizabeth Johnson states is valid, that "we are united with God in Jesus by being in compassionate solidarity with those who suffer" (Johnson 2010, 126), then a question that arises is: how effective is theological reflection that does not consciously encourage a stance of solidarity? Parable as a lens for theological reflection keeps the dialogue focused on the question of solidarity and the steps necessary to build those relationships of trust and compassion.

Our first chapter focused on the presupposition that God is present throughout our lives, and in the second chapter we posited that theological reflection is most effective when done in a communal setting and when participants have a stance that is open to transformation. In this chapter we put forth a few more presuppositions that frame our thinking about parables. Parables have aspects that are familiar, aspects that are surprising or shocking, and they are open-ended—waiting for a response. In addition, parables point to the reign of God, and they do so by revealing a vision that is Good News for those on the margins. As we move into the fourth chapter, we will look at how parables offer a compelling lens to work alongside any method of theological reflection. By offering focus and direction, parables offer a helpful framework for reflecting theologically about the surprising nearness of God and the demands of that relationship.

NOTES

1. Christina Zaker, published in "Starting Point," *National Catholic Reporter*, August 31, 2007, Vol. 43, No. 35 edition, 4.

2. This and every scripture passage in this text are taken from *The Catholic Study Bible - New American Bible*, 2nd ed. (Oxford University Press, 2006).

Chapter 4

Exploring Parable as a Lens for Reflection

Key Frameworks for Reflective Practice

One morning while I sat developing my thinking around parables as a lens for reflection, my son Joshua, who was nine at the time, walked in and cuddled next to me. "What are you doing?" he asked. "My homework," I replied still lost in my own thoughts. He then asked, "Can I help?" I paused, thought for a moment and then said, "Sure. Tell me a story of anything that happened at school yesterday." While he was thinking about a story, his older brother, Micah, walked in to say good morning. He sat himself down to listen to Josh's story too. While Josh was telling his story, I jotted down three questions and handed them to Micah. Here is how the conversation unfolded:

Josh—"Yesterday we did a cool art project. I had to work with Daniel and we made this origami boat. Daniel wasn't goofing around at all and it looked really neat when we were done. The teacher said we could take the boats home and Daniel wanted to take it home, so I said he could."
Micah: "These are Mom's questions: What was familiar in your story?"
Josh: "Familiar?"
Micah: "You know, like what was just like you expected—what was normal?"
Josh: "Well, I always have to do art projects with Daniel because he sits next to me, and the teacher has him sit next to me because he goofs off a lot, and maybe she thinks I don't mind, but I do sometimes."
Micah: "What surprised you in the story?"
Josh: "Daniel didn't goof off at all—he was really into it . . . and the boat came out really cool."
Micah: "And you let Daniel take the boat home—that surprised me."
Josh: "Yeah I guess, but he really liked it."
Micah: "Can you see God in the surprise?"
   (A long pause)

Josh: "That's a hard one . . . I guess God helped Daniel because he got to enjoy art this time. And maybe God is in my teacher because she tries really hard to make fun projects."
Micah: "Maybe God was in you because you let Daniel have the boat."
Josh: "You think?"
Micah: "Yeah, that was nice."

As I watched my sons unfold this experience, I was struck by how simple the conversation was, yet how extraordinary. I was reminded of the many times my children's conversations or insights or curiosity have surprised me with the utter nearness of God. James and Evelyn Whitehead say that the task of "Christian ministry is the formation of reflective communities alive to the presence of God" (1995, 17). My experiences as a wife and mother have taught me that all of life is ministry, and we learn the most about faith and theology and reflection by living life. The laughter, the joy, the grief of God breaks through at so many moments, and if I am listening well and not caught in my own thoughts, then I can catch those glimpses of Grace that are profoundly nourishing.

So far we have laid the foundation for exploring parables as a lens for theological reflection. This chapter begins by framing how parables offer a framework for theological reflection and by raising some of the questions that help guide this thinking. The bulk of the chapter will highlight steps for utilizing parables as a lens for reflection. Any process of theological reflection begins with naming an experience and exploring it in dialogue with a community. Here we name those processes as the first two steps, and we take the time to talk about the importance of why we start this way. We will then highlight the threefold pattern of parables as a lens for reflection. This pattern starts with a familiar scene drawn from our life or ministry; we will look at what is familiar about the scene and how it connects to our various sources. We then continue by exploring the pieces of the story that are surprising or deal a shocking image of the reign of God that demands a new way of seeing. Finally, we will explore how this lens for theological reflection addresses the open-ended invitation nature of parables. By wrestling with the invitation to respond to this new vision, we integrate the reflective practice into how we live our lives. Throughout the chapter, a number of examples of this type of reflection are provided to help you imagine the possibilities for your own reflective practice.

I started with that story of my sons on a Saturday morning. The familiar spaces in our homes or in our lives are often the places that simple stories become parabolic invitations to move toward solidarity. The conversation between my sons surprised me with the interaction that they had in naming how they might see God and even how they might see God in each other. I resonate so much with what Pope Francis said when he preached on October 13, 2014, "Our God is a God of surprises." He went on to invite his listeners to consider the question, "Am I open to the God of surprises? Am I a person who stands still, or a person on a journey?" He is reminding us of the invitation to enter into a relationship with God, to be on a journey of transformation, and often these moments that surprise or shock us reveal God's vision for how we might be transformed.

STEPPING FORWARD

When I first began working with theological reflection, I spent about ten years facilitating groups of students in the Archdiocese of Chicago's Lay Ecclesial Ministry and Deaconate Formation programs. Following the Whitehead model described in their book, *Method in Ministry*, I would meet with groups five to six times a year over two years, explaining the method, facilitating reflection, and encouraging their use of theological reflection as a tool in ministry. During that time, I began to explore other methods of theological reflection and framed my thinking about parables, methods, and facilitation. This exploration has continued through my work as the director of Field Education at Catholic Theological Union. Theological reflection is a critical piece of all of our field education courses. The method of theological reflection in parabolic mode developed out of this exploration.

One consistent experience throughout has been that, although many of the participants in theological reflection were students in graduate schools of theology, when engaging the tradition as part of the method, they most often drew from the corpus of the Gospel stories of Jesus. Their familiarity with and the impact of the stories of Jesus' life and his parables seemed the best source for their reflections. Although this was an intriguing and curious note, Andrew Greeley in his book *The Catholic Imagination* offers an explanation:

> The origins and raw power of religion are at the imaginative (that is, experiential and narrative) level both for the individual and for the tradition. . . . None of the doctrines are less true than the stories. Indeed, they have the merit of being more precise, more carefully thought out, more ready for defense and explanation. But they are not where religion or religious faith starts, nor in truth where it ends. (Greeley 2001, 4)

Thus, even with their training in theology, my students showed that, as Greeley says, the raw power to experience our faith is in the imaginative stories. Theological reflection is a way to move beyond how you learn about God to how you experience and relate to God. As we noted in the first chapter and what Greeley seems to be suggesting here is that sacramental imagination is cultivated through the narratives of our lives. Theological reflection plays a role in cultivating and shaping those narratives.

As I worked toward my Ecumenical Doctor of Ministry, in addition to leading theological reflection groups, I also dug deeply into studying the Gospel parables and Catholic social teaching. As you can see from the last chapter, I fell in love with the parables and their movement. I also resonated with the way the parables narrowed the focus to issues of justice, solidarity, and community. Each of these areas of study continued to shape what became theological reflection in parabolic mode.

As part of my research, I was given the opportunity to work with employees at Mercy Home for Boys and Girls in Chicago, a residential program for at-risk youth. Their president, Fr. Scott Donahue, graciously invited me to host lunch hour reflections with interested staff members. Twenty-five employees agreed to meet regularly throughout one summer. The group was made up of full-time employees from a wide variety of religious and cultural backgrounds. I developed a step-by-step method of reflection to help guide them as they facilitated their own reflections in small groups of five. Six steps lead participants through a parabolic flow to explore where God's movements could be found in their daily lives, and to explore if that grace was inviting transformation. Appendix A has the quick reference guide that was given to Mercy Home employees in order to help facilitate the conversation. What follows is an explanation of each of the steps, and suggestions on how they can be used and adapted.

We have already discussed in the first three chapters what we would call the "presuppositions" of theological reflection in parabolic mode. They are:

1. God is present throughout our lives
2. Parables have a reference point of the "reign of God"
3. Parables offer Good News for the marginalized
4. Parables have aspects that are familiar, comforting, and that make sense
5. Parables have aspects that are surprising or shocking, and challenging
6. Parables are open-ended—waiting for a response
7. Theological reflection works best if we are open to the process
8. Theological reflection works best in a community willing to discern together and to challenge one another.

Discussing these eight presuppositions as part of an initial conversation helps the group prepare to reflect together. This allows the group to consider the pattern of the parables and the dynamic at play in their focus on bringing Good News. As you can see from the earlier chapters, there can be a number of different ways to discuss these presuppositions. You can simply discuss each one as part of the initial conversation or give more in-depth information, either from this book or from other sources that you find helpful to frame the conversation.

Another reason for beginning with the discussion of the presuppositions is to get the group interacting. This initial conversation helps to build the community dynamic before stepping into the reflective process. Having a conversation about the flow of parables and sacramental imagination are also formative insights that, depending on the group, might be entirely new concepts for them. The dialogue around the presuppositions gives everyone a chance to learn and ask questions. It also helps to introduce participants to how reflective dialogue takes place.

NAMING THE EXPERIENCE

Step one is *naming the experience*. Starting with the first foundational thought that God is present throughout our lives, participants are encouraged to explore any story from their life with aims to discern God's movements. Just as was mentioned in the second chapter, participants can name any experience and begin to frame it as a story. Questions such as "What were the beginning, middle, and end moments in the story?", "What feelings arose?" or "What thoughts crossed your mind?" help to dig deeper into the scene and to fill the story in with the details of the event. In addition to naming the experience, participants are asked to note ways in which the storyteller was an observer and ways he or she was an active participant in the experience.

As we look at the steps of this method, it might be helpful to have an example of one story to explore. A student was working in campus ministry at a high school, and we can use his story as an example to follow throughout this process:

> He was new to the school and was helping out as a chaperone on a one-day service project at the local nature center. The group of about 20 high school boys was tasked with moving wheelbarrows full of mulch to resurface the nature center's pathways. They had all of the tools they needed such as wheelbarrows, shovels, rakes, and work gloves. They also had water, which was critical since they were working in about 90-degree heat. As the campus minister worked filling wheelbarrows with mulch, some of the high school students would then move it down the path and spread it out. The campus minister noticed that many of the high school students were tired from the heat or sitting down and goofing around after only about an hour. He finished filling a wheelbarrow and wondered how he might motivate the students to keep at it, as they had several more hours of work before they were finished. While he was wondering, one of

the smallest students in the group stood up to move the wheelbarrow. The campus minister watched him walk away, wondered if he was strong enough to do this, and was not surprised when the student started to falter as he pushed along. Immediately an older student who was sitting down hopped up to lend a hand. Both boys walked together to move the wheelbarrow down the path. When they returned, they were chatting and laughing, and waited for the wheelbarrow to be filled again.

As we explore this story, we note the starting point is to simply name the experience or to tell the story. Here we have a story where we can see the campus minister who is both participant and observer. He is participating as he focuses on filling wheelbarrows and wonders how he will keep a group of teenagers that he barely knows focused on the work in 90-degree heat. He is also an observer as he notes the actions of the high school students—their need to rest, their goofing around rather than helping out. He also observes the two students who stepped up to help.

EXPLORING THE EXPERIENCE AS A COMMUNITY

Step two is exploring the experience as a community. Here the foundational thoughts on openness and community are important. As the story is presented, participants begin to explore the story and find ways they relate to this story in their own lives. The participant, who has offered the story for reflection, allows the whole community to explore and own the story. People can ask clarifying questions to help them flesh out a better understanding of the events and feelings that played a role in this experience. As they ask questions and explore the story, they begin to have more ownership of the story and how it relates to incidents in their own lives. This conversation also allows for the story to become something that everyone is invested in, and the original storyteller can release their hold on the experience and work as part of the community while they continue to explore it together. This distancing encourages the storyteller and the whole group to have fresh eyes for what insights might arise. In allowing one's own story to be explored by the whole group, the storyteller is both vulnerable and free; vulnerable through the exposure of their emotions and actions being critiqued by the group, but also free to explore what they might need to learn from the experience.

In the story shared above, the group discussion opened up as the participants asked clarifying questions that helped the campus minister articulate his feelings of awkwardness around the teenagers whom he barely knew and also a bit of frustration with the task and the heat. They surfaced questions about where the other chaperones were and what were some of the conversations taking place to engage the group. As they asked more questions about the situation, they began to explore their own "judgments" of the teenagers. They realized that they had critiqued the students in general, and even the two who did step up, seeing the first one as too tiny to move the wheelbarrow and the second one as too "cool" to help at first. The group explored the ways they resonated with this experience, especially around the issue of how to relate to teen boys in a ministerial context. In any process of exploring the story as a community, there may be clarifying questions asked throughout the reflective process; however, once all of the participants feel they have a clear understanding of the experience and the feelings that were a part of their perspectives on the experience, the group is then ready to move on to step three.

RECOGNIZING THE FAMILIAR

With a shared understanding of the experience, the group can begin to ask what is familiar about this experience. Recognizing the fourth presupposition that parables begin with a familiar scene drawn from everyday life, the group begins by asking questions aimed at recognizing what is familiar in their stories. The goal is to ask questions that begin to uncover our lenses and assumptions. The order or the questions are not predetermined, but the shaded boxes offer some suggestions for how to begin unpacking the familiar. Starting with these types of questions helps participants uncover what they consider their comfort zone, or the lenses that they use as they react to the story. Killen and deBeer talk about this as exploring our positions, attitudes, beliefs, opinions, and convictions (Killen and deBeer 1994, 74). Unpacking the way we normally see the experience, or why certain aspects are familiar, helps us to enter into the experience with an eye on connecting ourselves to the deeper narratives. In addition to asking what is familiar, we also ask questions that uncover insights from the different sources.

When considering the source of sacred texts, I like to say that any story we bring to the table can also be found in our sacred texts. Stories of hope or fear, oppression or triumph are all part of scriptures. When we lay our stories alongside those from scripture, we open up new avenues to wisdom. If the group shares the same faith, they may find it helpful to brainstorm parables or stories in their own sacred texts that are similar and offer a familiar lens to the experience being explored. If the group feels there is a nice connection between their story and one particular parable or scripture story, it can be helpful to read the scripture aloud and explore it in depth. They can begin to relate ways the experience and the scripture story are similar and different, making comparisons between characters, scenes, and actions. In interreligious groups, it is important to invite people to share sacred texts from their own faith tradition, and participants may draw comparisons between different texts. Sometimes this comparison provides new and intriguing insights. However, depending on how the discussion is going or the makeup of the group, making this connection is not necessary.

In fact, if the context warrants it, theological language is not necessary at all. This method can be adapted for use in spaces that are not explicitly theological. Depending on the group, it may be counterproductive to discuss faith, but reflective practice is still a critical tool for life, and parables as a lens still holds promises for nonreligiously focused groups. I will go into detail on that possibility in chapter 6 when we discuss adaptations of this method. But for now, we will assume a group that is open to exploring the theological and scriptural themes that might be familiar in the experience.

> Types of questions for "what is familiar" include:
> What do we observe as familiar in the experience?
> What is comfortable?
> What makes sense about the way people act or respond in this experience? Does my culture or context determine why this is familiar?
> What happens that is expected?

The second level of questions in this step of recognizing the familiar delves deeper by asking the "why" questions—why are these things familiar or comfortable? This step is where the participants put their story and the wider context into dialogue with traditions, sacred texts, and other sources from our context. With the example of the students moving mulch, we may consider turning to sources such as psychology to consider issues of belonging and risk among the teenagers, or questions of social justice and eco-spirituality to talk about the impact of service-learning opportunities on the students. This first step is similar to the Whiteheads' steps of attending and asserting or, as Killen and de Beer state, "Exploring the heart of the matter in conversation with the wisdom of the Christian heritage" (Killen and de Beer 1994, 74). By exploring the familiar elements in our stories, we begin to uncover the "why" questions that ask "why have things always been this way" or "what is the complacency implicit in the familiar and comfortable." Social analysis questions are great to ask when we explore what is familiar in this situation, not only to find out what we can know about this situation, but also to frame how we ask the "why" questions. Why have things always been this way? Why does money or power play such a role here? Asking the "why" questions uncovers the lenses we wear as well as the gaps that exist in how we engage the sources along with our experience.

In the story with the campus minister and the high school boys, the group discussed the familiarity of trying to figure out how to work with teenage boys in the context of ministry, and several of them shared their own familiarity with being awkward as teenagers. This in turn brought up feelings of not fitting in even now in the role as campus minister. They discussed their own assumptions and judgment of the boys, and the way society in the US context expects a lack of engagement with boys in this age group. Recent articles about engaging youth in their culture were brought up and discussed. They talked about being familiar with what it means to be new to a school and having to figure out what responsibilities they have for the mission of their ministry. And they considered the familiar pressure of planning, supporting, encouraging, and modeling what a day of service could mean for community-building between the teens and the school community. They even considered the fact that they, too, would not have wanted to be there and working in the 90-degree heat.

In addition, they looked at what was similar between this story and the scriptures and traditions. This brainstorming process raised issues as varied as the sacrament of Confirmation, the corporeal works of mercy and Catholic social teaching. They discussed the familiar scene of "mandatory volunteer" days through school and what types of messages they send. When looking at the scriptures, they saw similarities in this story to a number of different scriptures, but settled on exploring more deeply Matthew 21: 28–32, the parable of the man who had two sons. As they explored this parable in light of the story that had been brought to the table, they saw the contrasts between showing up to work and not doing the task at hand. But as they explored their story alongside the scripture story, they slowly began to appreciate another theme to the story that surprised and challenged them—we'll talk about that in the next section.

This process of digging deeply into one's own assumptions allows participants to question why they respond the way they do or why they respond the way parents, peers, or society expects them to. By mining our understanding of and familiarity with an experience, we begin to expose and open ourselves up to the gaps we have in our understanding, including the ways we can still learn and begin to analyze whether or not that familiar is something that needs to be critiqued. If the group gathered comes from different cultures, the answers to these questions are likely to be very different, as different cultures find different experiences as familiar. We begin to broaden our lenses by first uncovering what we consider familiar and then learning what others at the table consider familiar, too. Once the group has explored what the comfort zone of their story is, they are then ready for step four.

> Some examples of questioning why things are familiar include:
> Why do these responses make sense? Are they based on past experiences, on the way things are simply always done, or on the expectations people or the society have?
> Why does our society or culture respond in this way?
> Why is it important that things are done in this way?

SEEKING THE SURPRISE

Based on the presupposition that parables always have a surprising or shocking twist, the questions in step four invite theological reflectors to explore ways this experience, or our reflection on this experience, offers a surprising twist. Sometimes as we explore our questions and our sources, the elements of surprise happen in the midst of our reflection on the story rather than within the story itself.

> Questions that help explore the surprise or shocking parts of the story include:
> What do we observe as surprising in this experience?
> What was uncomfortable?
> What happened that was not what we expected?
> What challenged us because it turned our expectations upside down?
> Did our own actions surprise us?

Inevitably, toward the start of a semester in my theological reflection classes, one student will always name their surprise at the process itself; when we unpacked the familiar of the story, they were amazed at the breadth and depth of the connections they were able to make to a simple story. This surprise shows how participants are expanding their ability to imagine and connect their story to their tradition and context. It also reveals how the Spirit works in a group gathered in reflection. The wealth of new insights and perspectives is one way to see God's surprising nearness, but it is also good to challenge participants to keep digging into the story itself.

As in step three, the questions can move from those that name observations to ones that ask for a deeper explanation. These "why" questions aim to raise fundamental insights. They prod us to consider where we might need to see things in a new way, or how we might be asked to critique our actions in the incident or the status quo that impacts our responses. Insights and wisdom can also be found in the contrasting questions, too. If we look at the story and find nothing surprising or challenging, we might ask, "Why not?" It is also helpful to ask the why and why not questions in the comparison between the experience and the scriptures. We might ask how the surprises of the story are similar or different from those found in the parables, or what is the new vision that is being offered in this surprise.

> Sample "Why" questions to the surprises include:
> Why were these pieces surprising or shocking?
> How does this moment of surprise challenge my thinking about the way things are or could be?
> Where have the expectations of other people or the culture been turned upside down?
> Asking contrast questions can also lead to wisdom: if you feel that nothing happened that was shocking, why not?
> Are you looking deeply enough?
> What should be happening to reveal God's presence there?
> Should something shocking have happened?

Returning to our example of the campus minister and the students moving mulch; when we began to ask "what surprised you here," generally the response was that the boy who was small in stature was first to step up and help without being asked. They also named a surprise as the moment the campus minister watched as the student faltered and another student jumped up to steady the wheelbarrow and offer a hand. There were also surprises in the fact that, rather than simply take the wheelbarrow from the smaller teen, the two of them together moved it down the path.

The moment of surprise in an experience is often where there is a subtle crack in the storyline for God to break in and invite a new vision. I like to say that the moment of surprise is the moment we are parabled! Surprise provides the opportunity to be disoriented enough to momentarily see something we would otherwise miss. Surprises are the moments we catch a glimpse of the reign of God. When the group looked at the story of moving mulch in light of the parable of the two sons, the surprising challenge that began to percolate in the conversation around the table was the question of what job the campus minister really was there to do. Had he focused so much on the task of moving the mulch that he had forgotten about his role to engage the students and build community? As the conversation continued, they admitted that this was a chance for him to get to know the students a little better, and yet it was perhaps a missed opportunity because he chose to act out of his own awkwardness and focus on moving mulch more than on building community. They all agreed that this was probably what each of them would have focused on, but they explored the reasons why that would have been their response. When the students studied this story alongside the parable, they began to be challenged by the notion that perhaps they were the "sons" who said "yes father" and yet did not do the work asked of them, while the high school students were the ones who might have initially said "no," and yet in the end were the ones who modeled how to build and sustain community. This surprising new shift in the vision of the story leads into the fifth step.

ACKNOWLEDGING THE INVITATION

Step five is acknowledging the invitation. This step is rooted in the parabolic pattern that sees the new vision presented in the parable as an invitation to respond. The hunch is that the moments of surprise or shock reveal where God is inviting growth and transformation. Participants are being invited to open up and respond to a new vision. Just as in the parables there are items that are surprising and reveal a new way to experience or understand the reign of God, the moments of surprise in our own experiences can reveal God's movement or invitation. As we look to the invitation, we again see that there are two perspectives to consider when reflecting on the experience: one as an observer and one as a participant. These perspectives correlate with two of the foundational presuppositions: parables point to the reign of God, and they are always Good News for those on the margins. In our stories, we can observe the reign of God revealed in the scene, and our actions or the way we respond clarify our willingness to participate in the Good News.

> Some examples of invitational questions include:
> How is the moment of surprise a moment where the experience reveals God's presence or God's invitation?
> What insights do the surprises in the experience give to our understanding of God?
> What about the experience challenges or invites a response?
> How might this experience encourage a new way of seeing the situation?
> How might this experience be an invitation into a relationship with God?
> In what ways do the pieces of this experience that are uncomfortable or shocking shed light on ways we are supposed to challenge our understanding of the context?
> How might the authority of our experience provide a challenge to the sources of tradition, scripture, or context?
> Who or what showed the movement of God in the similar parable and how might that reveal a new way to envision the experience?

Exploring Parable as a Lens for Reflection 75

As an observer, participants are encouraged to see where God moves in the experience and to see or recognize the reign of God revealed in the actions of the others. The questions asked in this step help the group begin to see in the moments of surprise God's movement and surprising nearness. This step offers the opportunity to be challenged by the vision of the reign of God that breaks through in the moments of surprise.

In the story of the campus minister and the high school students moving mulch, there was an easy correlation in observing God at work in the two students who stepped up to help and in their supporting one another to get the job done. God is in the new friendships starting to form and in how they modeled a willingness to keep working despite the heat when they initially did not have the right "stuff" to undertake the task. In the reign of God, we show up—imperfect as we may be—and together (with God) we have enough to get the job done.

From the stance of a participant in the experience, the participants are encouraged to see themselves in the story and realize how their actions respond to God. Through this series of questions, the group is encouraged to appreciate how their actions were (or were not) Good News for those on the margins. The work of justice and solidarity comes through in this part of the conversation. Examining the experience with an eye for what reveals a just response or what builds right relationships are ways that participants uncover how their actions are a response to God's invitation to a new vision of justice. Participants not only explore the actions that took place in the experience, but also how their reflections can shape their actions to bring Good News in the future or how they collaborate in building up the reign of God. This reflective dialogue cultivates the space to note God at work in their shared reflection, too.

> Questions that highlight the Good News at work include:
> How do the actions that take place exemplify the Good News?
> How could the actions have been more surprising or more in line with the Good News?
> How are the actions a response to the invitation into relationship with God?
> How do the things that were surprising in the experience invite a way to nurture the Good News?
> Where was the Good News in the similar parable? How is that Good News similar to or different from the experience of this story?"

In the story with the campus minister and the high school students, the discussion raised the question: "How did the campus minister participate in building the reign of God?" They acknowledged that he focused on the task at hand (moving the mulch), which probably helped to keep the students motivated, but they also considered what was the real "task" in the vision of God. By asking how those in the experience could have done more to bring the Good News in the context of this story, the discussion returned again to the parable of the two sons. There they considered the task God asked of each "son" in their story. They made a comparison between the campus minister as the first son who said "yes" to his father's request to go work, and the two students who moved the wheel barrel together as the second son who initially said "no." In doing this, they considered how the campus minister said yes to moving mulch, but got lost in the task and neglected to focus on the task of building community and making connections with the students. If the expectation was to simply move the mulch, then the task was accomplished; if the expectation of the campus minister was to build relationships and community, then perhaps he fell short of the task. Likewise, students who were sitting around and goofing off were initially saying "no" to the task at hand, yet in the end the two who stepped up to help showed the collaborative realm of God's grace.

The theological reflection group spent time exploring these insights and appreciated that the campus minister was willing to be vulnerable within the group which allowed all of them to own the response honestly. Through their discussion they talked about how sometimes initial responses, even for campus ministers, are rooted more in those feelings of fear, judgment, or awkwardness that were so much a part of the high school experience. Those feelings, it seemed to the group, were not helpful in collaborating with God, and all acknowledged that awareness of those feelings as underlying motivations helped each of them as participants to recognize the invitation to growth and transformation.

The surprise in the story might be different for everyone. Different people may notice different points of surprise and be challenged by different invitations. Each participant is encouraged to discover the surprising, challenging, or shocking element for him or herself and to explore what the invitation might be in that surprise. With my students in our ministry practicum theological reflection, we ask each participant to name their surprise in the story and the way they see that as an invitation. Generally, I have to remind them to use first-person language so that they own the invitation and see it as something for their own personal growth. But in some cases the group as a whole needs to discern a response.

In a setting where a group is discussing an issue that they would like to solve together, the conversation might look different than simply naming our surprise and invitation to respond. If a parish council is discerning how to develop a ministry for domestic violence in their community, the conversation may have surfaced a number of possible responses. Here the group will need to prayerfully discern together each of their own surprises as well as the challenges presented to the whole group in order to determine the essential paths forward. The pastor may be surprised by the number of people who showed up for the conversation, a parish council member might be surprised by the statistics that show domestic violence is an issue in every community, and the parishioner who is a lawyer might be surprised by the fact that her expertise is valued in this conversation. Another might feel like he finally has a safe place to share his own experience of intimate partner violence. In each of these surprises we see an invitation to hope and to grow. With each person there is a personal invitation—for one it might be to be hopeful about the positive response or the sacred space being formed, for another it might be trusting to find their voice or share their expertise, while for another it might be the invitation to learn and listen. The group as a whole will also want to discern how they as a community respond. The hope and willingness to share, listen, and create a sacred space gives them the permission to do a richer social analysis of the situation of domestic violence in their congregation and the surrounding community. This reflective process over time cultivates a parish response that is rooted in God's invitation to be Good News.

The surprises always lead to a perspective that our response can be Good News to those who have been marginalized. Sometimes the focus is on responding to systemic oppression, other times the Good News happens in our own hearts when we are transformed by hope and hospitality rather than by our own judgments and fears. This perspective—that doing theology is fundamentally tied up with a perspective from the margins—is not a new one. Liberation theology, feminist theology, womanist theology, and others have all attempted to get the attention of the centers of power when claiming their right to have a voice. Pope Francis has moved in this direction with his plea for the church to become a field hospital among his other actions that privilege the experiences of those on the margins. What is critical for this study is how we shape theological reflection that encourages participants, even those who stand closer to the centers of power, to pay attention to how they participate in the marginalization of others and to take a stance that is parabolic. As Hoffsman Ospino points out, "To opt preferentially for the poor demands that we humbly accept our complicity as society and faith communities in the conditions that lead many people to live in poverty and marginalization" (2010, 426). The parabolic method helps participants recognize a new vision not from a position of oppression in need of liberation, but to recognize where they hold a position of power and need to dismantle the ways they "other" someone else. This perspective, or being able to see with new eyes, helps participants to take steps to move toward the margins and respond to the invitation. This movement to the margins is important to all people of faith.

Chapter 4

RESPONDING TO THE INVITATION

Theological reflection through the lens of parables began by exploring an experience to glimpse the vision of the reign of God and possible ways to participate in its advent. The next step moves to discerning a response to that invitation. Participants are invited to internalize and integrate the reflection and consider how they might respond to the insights gained. The invitation is to recognize the actions that could be different the next time or to recognize God's movement more readily in the daily moments of Grace. In addition, participants are challenged to consider how they might voice critique or challenge to the prevailing theologies or societal expectations. As the group reflects on the insights generated, they are each encouraged to articulate concrete ways they might begin to integrate those insights into their lives. By asking participants to name a concrete response, there is a better chance that they will embrace the invitation and act on it in the future.

> Questions that help formulate a response include:
> What insights or challenges will you hold onto from this reflection?
> How will this reflection impact your actions in the future?
> How does this reflection help you to recognize God in the midst of the world?
> How can you name ways you might respond to God with your life?
> Based on this reflection, what needs to change—in society, in the way we understand the scriptures, in our own lives—and what should we do to move toward that change?
> How do we as individuals and as a community celebrate the responses that are Good News?
> How do we see ourselves as collaborating in building the Reign of God?
> Name concrete ways your actions or observations will be influenced by this reflection.

The nature of theological reflection in a communal setting is that the action responses are not something we accomplish while sitting around the discussion table. The time spent in dialogue, asking questions, and listening to one another in theological reflection around the table is where we cultivate the ground enabling such insights to take root. Concrete actions and communal responses are discussed and named, and hopefully committed to, and even planned out during theological reflection. Thus, articulating possible responses helps participants to build their commitment to actually living out their new vision. Going a step further to formulate action steps, timelines, or accountability goals are all steps that could be taken by a group using this tool to plan together or individuals making a commitment within the process to respond to the invitation.

LENS RATHER THAN METHOD

The lens of parable was partly designed out of a desire to imagine theological reflection that was a simple process rather than a cumbersome method to follow. Having led theological reflection over a number of years, employing a variety of methods, I could see how a group could easily get lost in the method or steps and lose focus on the main goal. Theological reflection is about discerning the presence of God in everyday experience. This discernment is not, however, only about recognizing God in the world but also about seeking to understand how we enter into a relationship with God and discern the demands of that relationship. This is the core goal of theological reflection, and most methods have language that suggests they recognize this fundamental dynamic in their thinking. However, in putting each method to use, facilitators and participants can fail to remember this dynamic while they focus on the details of the steps. Practitioners can be so focused on the steps of the method that they fail to remember that the Spirit is at work in the midst of the reflective moment. This discrepancy in implementation can lead to a frustration with theological reflection as a whole. As Pattison notes, "While professional theological educators see TR as the jewel in their disciplinary crown, a good number of their students regard this activity as an irritating and inhibiting pebble in the ministerial shoe" (Pattison, Thompson, and Green 2003, 127). Parable as a lens for theological reflection offers a simpler way to keep focus throughout the shared reflection. By keeping in mind the parabolic flow, the reflection not only moves through the steps easily, but the surprising nature keeps participants aware of the moments of Grace as well.

Only three key questions drive the direction of the reflection process through the lens of parables. These three questions are aligned with the same pattern that is evident in the flow of parables. By remembering to ask, "What is familiar?", "What is surprising?", and "What is the invitation?" participants are able to keep track of where they are in the discussion and be open to how the Spirit moves the conversation. Depending on the direction the conversation takes, each facilitator or participant can nuance the discussion by asking a variety of questions such as those suggested in the steps above. The third question "What is the invitation?" can also be more specifically asked: "How does the surprise reveal God's invitation?" or "How is this new vision an invitation to collaborate with God's Good News?" All of these questions keep the focus clearly on understanding the new vision and response presented through the reflection.

The story of my sons at the beginning of this chapter followed this simple process. Although in that example only the three main questions were asked, it still offered the encouraging insights of a big brother naming the actions of his younger brother as an image of God or a student recognizing God in the efforts of his teacher. Theological reflection conversations generally take more time than simply asking those three questions. Knowing the distinction of the three movements to the discussion offers a framework that is simple to follow even in the depth it provides; however, if the facilitator does not keep an eye on the flow and the overall goals, any method can get lost in the "what is the familiar" conversation. Plenty of discussions have been rich and varied as we attended to the various contextual, scriptural, and tradition sources. The discussion may have even encouraged participants to consider how they will do things differently in the future. However, if the facilitator and the group as a whole fail to identify *why* they are exploring the sources or what this exploration is providing by way of a new vision of the Reign of God, then they may just circle around in the conversation without moving forward. By utilizing the threefold pattern in parables as a lens, the reflective process continues forward by seeking out the moments of parabolic *metanoia*, or transformation, that are critical to theological reflection.

Let us take a look again at the definition of theological reflection: theological reflection at its best is a communal effort to discern God's presence in the world, to carve the space for that presence to invite us into a new vision, and to lay the groundwork for that new vision to take root in how we live our lives. The parabolic flow is evident in the effort to discern God's presence in the familiar stuff of the world, to be surprised by a new vision that is presented when we discern God's nearness, and to allow that new vision to invite us into a way of living that is a surprising response.

I would like to offer one reflection shared with the group of employees at Mercy Home for Boys and Girls as a fresh example of theological reflection through the lens of parable and its three-part movement.

> One of the employees wanted to do something nice for one of the residents of Mercy Home, so she took him for a bike ride through the city. The harried pace of biking through crowded city streets amongst loud and haphazard taxis left her heart pounding, but the casual look on the resident's face captured her attention. He was familiar with this frantic pace and zigzagged among the taxis without fear. As they relaxed at a park fountain before embarking on the trip home, the worker was struck by the quality of the conversation with the resident as he shared his bag of popcorn with her.

The group reflected together on this story and found "familiar" pieces not only in the social analysis questions that gave perspective on the young people in their care, but also around issues of race, economics, and education.[1]

They also focused on the familiar pieces of being in the city and its frantic pace, the desire to see going for a bike ride as a gift of time, the effort on her part to reach out and offer companionship to one of the at-risk teens with whom she ministers, as well as her feeling out of place in the city while the resident felt very much at home and uninhibited by the chaos. Her coworkers shared similar feelings of attempting to reach out and/or feelings of being out of place as they tried to make a difference for the residents.

They also noted the familiar occurrence of getting into more meaningful conversations with residents outside of the normal routines and spaces. They began to surface questions around issues of chaos and calm, and why conversations with residents were often more comfortable and confiding at oases or places out of the normal routines. The image from scripture that surfaced during the reflection was of Jesus walking on water in the midst of the storm and Peter attempting, but then failing, to trust in Jesus' invitation to join him on the water (Matthew 25:22–33). This was the strongest image that surfaced for them, although they also considered the concepts of Eucharist with the sharing of food intertwined with the sharing of life, the notion of retreat or oasis, and other scriptures such as the parable of the good shepherd seeking out the one lost sheep.

When reflecting on what was surprising, the participant was challenged by the notion that although she was "helping" him, it was the resident that reflected God's presence for her. The notion of vulnerability on the bike ride, sharing of food and rich conversation at the fountain, and both having something to share with and learn from the other brought out a discussion of solidarity and standing with those on the margins. It also brought into acute focus the "surprising" image of the resident's calm in the city traffic. This image resonated as they explored the image of Jesus walking on water, and they noted how it invited the coworkers to consider what it means for them to step out of the boat like Peter and trust enough to walk toward the other. This is essentially a reality of their work; it pushes them out of their comfort zone every day. But to recognize the residents themselves as Jesus inviting them out of their comfort zone, rather than as Peter in need of their mercy, was startling and invited more reflection.

When they explored the invitation that was raised through this surprise, they reminded themselves of the reality that work in these settings would always be filled with moments of calm and moments of chaos. They reminded themselves that the time they take to learn from the young people in their care is just as important as the work they do to make their dinners or help them do their homework. They acknowledged that both types of accompaniment fostered hope and confidence and solidarity. Each of the co-workers walked away considering the unique ways they might respond concretely to the invitation to see Christ in their residents—but not Christ in need of assistance, rather Christ as the companion beckoning them out of the boat of their comfort zones.

STYLE, METHOD, LENS

This form of theological reflection could line up with Kinast's taxonomy of styles in a number of different places. The example of the reflection with the coworkers at Mercy Home could be considered a ministerial style reflection because it took place in the context of ministry and helped the participants to reframe their ministerial identity. But the reflection was not around a ministerial issue that needed a response. It was more a reflection on something that had happened in the day-to-day movement of life, not a problem to be solved. With this in mind, parable as a lens could also be considered a spiritual wisdom style of theological reflection because it works from the sacramental imagination and hopes to develop the wisdom that comes from glimpses of Grace in our everyday experiences. Because this method insists that the reflection consider the invitation or the demands made by the new vision, it could be considered a praxis or practical method. I would also suggest it could fall under the liberative lens in its willingness to see parables as a critique that flips expectations on their heads. This happens in the story when the at-risk youth is seen in the position of Jesus who calmly beckons those in power—steering the boat—to leave that behind and risk vulnerability in a relationship.

In a sense, theological reflection in parabolic mode is not so much a specific style or method of theological reflection; rather, it offers a focused movement for any reflective practice. By keeping the simple pattern in mind, "What's familiar, what's surprising, how is that an invitation to Good News," any of life's moments can be reflected upon and broken open in new ways. This is what Pope Francis is suggesting when he asks: "Am I open to the God of surprises? Am I a person who stands still, or a person on a journey?"

WILLING TO BE SURPRISED

Pope Francis' question is an important one to ask any person of faith. Are we willing to be moved by God's surprising nearness? Are we able to move out of our comfort zone? Are we willing to be parabled? As I worked on developing theological reflection through the lens of parables, I kept coming back to the question of whether or not theological reflection is effective if it does not challenge our vision of the world or raise questions about our responsibility to respond to the needs of those around us. Reid points out, "Jesus' parables proclaim that God is not neutral. Rather, God is always on the side of those who are poorest and most oppressed" (Reid 2000, 10). If this is a valid understanding of God in the context of Jesus' parables, then it might be important to ask the question of whether or not theological reflection is effective if it remains neutral to the voice of the oppressed.

This is a primary consideration as we look at the cultural context of power and privilege in the United States. James Cochrane in his book, *Circles of Dignity* "privileges struggle as a locus of knowledge of considerable importance for theology" (1999, 23). His belief is that struggle and transformation of worldview is critical for doing theology. With this insight, I found myself asking, does marginalization and struggle increase the theological wisdom of believers? If the ordinary believer in the United States does not necessarily view their faith through a liberative lens, are they able to do theology well? One reality is that, within mainstream US culture, vulnerability is not an acceptable characteristic. Dick Westley suggests, "The individualism of our cultural upbringing makes community look like weakness, giving the impression that one does not have what it takes to 'stand alone'" (Westley 1992, 40). The US mainstream, as Thomas Rausch highlights, is a "culturally post-Christian, individualistic, mass-consumer society" (2010, 146). Rauch notes that sociologist Robert Wuthnow believes that modern spiritualities that are not rooted in an organized religion, but calling for transformation "provide ready-made answers for the small setbacks and petty anxieties of ordinary life but do not speak of a righteous God who demands anything of believers" (Rausch 2010, 148).

If these theories of the US contextual and religious landscape are close to accurate, then how does one encourage a stance that privileges real struggle not just the "small setbacks and petty anxieties" of life? As Ospino claims, "Accompaniment as preferential option for the poor means to literally, share the suffering that destroys the lives of poor women and men in our society" (2010, 426–427). Theological reflection in parabolic mode encourages this type of reflection and move to solidarity. This lens keeps the effort focused on God's surprising moves to critique and expose complacency and the invitation to respond. When we engage in reflection that actively seeks the voice of those on the margins, it is hard to remain neutral, to not see with eyes that can see.

However, the lens of parables offers more than a structural lens for theological reflection: it offers a philosophical lens as well. Donahue points out, "Jesus himself *is* parable; so also the Gospel presentations of him. Thus, theological language is radically parabolic" (Donahue 1998, 10). In this light, parables offer theological reflection the idea of beginning with common experiences and moving to exploring the world through the parabolic lens open to how it might shatter or shock. Parables interpret life; this perspective suggests that a parabolic lens for reflecting will offer insight and critique. The critique is not only of those sitting around the table, but of their worldviews and the structures that shape the world itself. Beyond exposing participants to the voice of the other, we also must ask how those voices challenge our relationship to God. The vision exposed in and through parables interprets, critiques, or shatters the old vision and invites reflection and response. Being drawn into the parable, shocked by its critique, and left free to respond offers a fresh vision for theological reflection.

Chapter 4

THE QUESTION OF SOLIDARITY

A question that keeps surfacing in this work is, "Why is it important for any of us to engage theological reflection? If the critique offered by this lens of parabolic reflection is challenging and tough, why would we want to do it at all?" I would like to suggest that it is necessary to be reflective people open to solidarity. The notion of solidarity is something that is far more complex than can be covered in this text, but for a quick reference, we will look to the definition of solidarity offered in *On Social Concern*, paragraph 38, "[Solidarity] then is not a feeling of vague compassion or shallow distress at the misfortunes of so many people both near and far. On the contrary, it is a firm and persevering determination to commit oneself to the common good; that is to say to the good of all and of each individual, because we are all really responsible for all" (1987, #38). Solidarity is a rich part of Catholic social teaching, and it encourages the perspective that we live fully our role in the Body of Christ by being in tune to the lives and struggles of those around us. Larry Snyder shares the view that the perspective of those at the margins is of value theologically and socially when he states:

> The basic question before us is what kind of a society we want to be. We are a creative, talented, and gifted people who are rich in resources. If we put our minds to it, we can reshape the social contract of our country so that no person is left out or left behind. We should not be content with maintaining the status quo. To bring about the dramatic change that reflects our faith and commitment, we need to "think and act anew." (Snyder 2010, 114)

His call to "think and act anew" encourages people of faith to not only expand their knowledge of and relationship with those on the margins, but also to explore how their faith and their salvation is bound together in solidarity with those on the peripheries of power.

Throughout the development of this lens for theological reflection, parables kept narrowing the focus of theological reflection to the question of solidarity. Somehow, in the attempt to narrow the focus through parable, I kept coming back to the question of whether or not solidarity was a core narrative of this "new vision" within theological reflection. Questions of who has a voice, or who is capable of theological reflection, or statements about including the voice of the marginalized or the subversive nature of the parables themselves kept surfacing. I found myself asking, "What does solidarity have to do with theological reflection?" Does this question keep surfacing because my own lens seeks it out, or because the parable lens provides a provocative focus on it?

Holland and Henriot offer some thoughts regarding solidarity. Through their pastoral spiral method they suggest, "In order to respond effectively to situations of injustice in today's world and to people's related spiritual hunger, we must strive to understand the social reality in all its complexities" (1985, 89). Not only are they suggesting a method of social analysis that drives at understanding these complexities, but they go on to state that the future of theological reflection in the United States needs to move in this direction as well. "To be frank, the theological reflection we need is difficult to find in North America . . . the North American theological community is confronted by two major tasks: (1) to forge a strong link between theology and social science; and (2) to link the theological process with the experience of the poor and oppressed" (1985, 93). Parable as a lens imagines a way of reflecting that attends to both of those major tasks.

Along the same lines, Schillebeeckx points out, "Now, in the Jesus Christ of the churches, the concern is almost exclusively with the person of the prophet, while we are silent about his message, often misunderstand it and distort it while nevertheless calling ourselves Christians" (*God Among Us*, 43). Herzog concurs stating, "Justice was at the center of Jesus' spirituality. It is the conceit of the North American church that Jesus was not involved in politics and economics but limited himself to spiritual matters" (1994, 264). Elizabeth Johnson most poignantly summarizes:

> "There is a traditional axiom, which claims that to live a good ethical life one must "do good and avoid evil." The emphasis shifts today, slightly but very dramatically, to make us realize that this is not enough. In fact, it can end up being a shirking of responsibility. For in the light of the compassion of God revealed in Jesus, we must 'do good and resist evil.'" There is a call to the Christian conscience here not to hide our face from evil, not to walk around it, or pretend it is not there; but to face its massiveness in spite of our feelings of powerlessness or insignificance and to become involved in transforming it. Suffering people are the privileged place where the God of compassion is found." (1990, 126)

While each of these theologians are encouraging the notion that the voices of the marginalized must be engaged with, they also seem to claim that we have a responsibility as people of faith to be in solidarity with those on the margins. It is in this solidarity that we most clearly experience Christ's mission of healing, embracing, and offering dignity. Similarly, the Whiteheads expose why the notion of solidarity might be avoided when they comment, "As long as . . . ('God's in his heaven; all's right with the world'), there is no special need for reflection and the purification it brings. Otherness—in the face of the poor and the sick and the outcast—interjects tension into our shared life of faith" (1995, 50). All of these voices seem to suggest that part of entering into the reflective process means opening ourselves up to the critique that parable and God's vision can offer, which is one fundamentally tied to humanity in communion with one another. Solidarity based in justice is about being in a right relationship to God and to the world around us.

Cochrane suggests what he sees as critical to the task of including or recovering more voices: we must distinguish "between conversation (dialogue) and collaboration (solidarity). Collaboration takes the form of a commitment to a partner who may not be equal in respect of access to and use of power" (1999, 169). This distinction between dialogue and solidarity offers a critique of theological reflection that sets out only to have a dialogue. Here he seems to suggest that dialogue is not enough to include the voice of the other, it is only the beginning. Jesus' parables and his lived experience suggest solidarity across multiple uneven divides of power. Perhaps too, theological reflection utilizing the lens of parable suggests solidarity more than dialogue, or parabolic living more than problem solving.

Being "parabled," as Crossan first suggested, or surprised by God means being willing to "see with eyes that can see" and to be on the journey toward the reign of God. Theological reflection through the lens of parable means carving out the space, opening up to this surprising vision and responding in a way that collaborates in God's Good News. This response brings us more deeply into community and solidarity.

Throughout this chapter we explored several different stories. There was the simple conversation between my two sons, the sustained exploration of the campus minister and the story of a bike ride through the streets of Chicago. In each story there were familiar scenes, surprising moments of Grace and invitations to sustained building of right relationships. Each story revealed insights that were Good News. Perhaps the Good News was the recognition of God in the face of the other, or the invitation to renewed efforts to build community, or the summons to move even further out of our comfort zone into solidarity. Each offered a glimpse of what it means to be parabled. Theological reflection is about having these conversations and being moved to respond in surprising ways. Theological reflection is a deeply spiritual exercise and our next chapter will explore the intersection of theological reflection as a spiritual practice.

NOTE

1. Holland and Henriot's or Cimperman's *Social Analysis* questions are examples of the types of questions that help unpack the familiar in what we know about a situation, or what we could learn in order to analyze it more fully. The economics and historical setting to the political and structural influences all play a role in understanding the context. For a more thorough look at social analysis and the questions that help build an understanding of the familiar through a contextual lens, see especially Cimperman's *Social Analysis for the 21st Century*, pp. 99–110.

Chapter 5

Connecting

Reflective Practice, Solidarity, and the Spiritual Life

Some time ago, my husband and I watched a "60 Minutes" episode focused on the amount of marketing brands children are exposed to daily in the United States. At the time we had children between the ages of four and eleven and were appalled by the data on the pervasiveness of branding in children's lives. This was before any of them had exposure to iPads or smart phones, so I can only imagine that the exposure for today's children is even more pervasive. After that episode, we had a conversation with our children about the show, and together we decided to figure out how we could "out brand" the brands. We talked about what was our family brand and how we wanted to make sure we had more of our brand visible throughout our house. The children thought items like crosses or statues, as well as pictures of cousins and their school art projects, were all considered our "family brand." Then we went around the house, removed as many branded items as possible, and where we couldn't, we made sure that we had more of our brand present in each room. So, in the kitchen with its multiple "Whirlpool" and "KitchenAid" images, we hung a cross and covered the fridge with pictures. We did that for each room and also initiated the effort to leave all shoes (and their various "swish" branding) by the front door so that we didn't have a multitude of brand images strewn across the house. Of course, I liked that idea for other reasons, but since the kids brought it up, I wholeheartedly agreed!

That conversation and the subsequent flurry of activity to define our family brand stuck with us through the years. The kids still take their shoes off at the front door, picture frames get updated as the cousins grow, and although the artwork has changed over the years, the fridge still holds images that I am happy to claim as our brand. Perhaps the children do not even remember that first conversation, but the taste of it lingers in the patterns that have shaped the way we are a family and value faith. That conversation and those activities are an example of an elementary spiritual practice of simplicity and a celebration of what we value and love. It started with a feeling of dissonance, was reflected on in a conversation with the family, and compelled the whole group to action that became embedded into the patterns of life. This example is similar to patterns in spiritual practices that we will touch on in this chapter.

In the first four chapters of this book we examined theological reflection. First, we considered the claims of the Catholic imagination that God is present in all things and throughout history, even in our most mundane moments of life. With this presupposition, we explored how theological reflection is a tool used to attune our hearts to God's presence. We have traced the pattern of how our theological reflection, and particularly with theological reflection through the lens of parables, highlights God's surprising nearness and the invitation to transformation and solidarity.

This chapter will adjust the lens ever so slightly to explore how theological reflection itself is a spiritual practice. We will begin by defining spirituality, spiritual practices, and vocation on a hunch that theological reflection as a spiritual practice transforms our spiritual lives and shapes our vocational direction. Next, we will explore a couple of well-regarded spiritual practices to draw comparisons between them and theological reflection. We will narrow our focus on the role of dialogue in spiritual practices and then highlight dialogue, and particularly the dialogue necessary for the lens of parables, as the critical piece of theological reflection that leads to solidarity and transformation. My hope is that this chapter demonstrates that theological reflection is a spiritual practice that integrates our spirituality and our daily life, bound by a communal effort toward solidarity and hope.

DEFINING SPIRITUALITY

One summer afternoon when our family was camping in the Adirondack Mountains in New York, we were caught in a downpour that showed no signs of letting up. Rather than trying to keep four little ones occupied in a soggy canvas tent, we loaded into the car and headed to the nearest town. To our relief we found a Barnes & Noble bookstore, and we spent the afternoon lost in good books and comfy chairs. As I wandered the shelves, I found my way to the "spirituality" section and had to laugh at how sparsely filled the section was and that the books there were about crystals and tarot card readings. Not one book referenced a relationship to God. I realized that, in this selection, "new age" spirituality seemed the most tangible form of otherworldliness. Yet I was saddened because spirituality has so much depth and the near empty shelves seemed starved of the richness of spirituality and all its complexities. This gaping hole in the spiritual inventory at the local Barnes & Noble seemed to point to the need for the wider public to understand and define spirituality in tangible language.

Ronald Rolheiser offers a definition of spirituality at the beginning of his text, *Holy Longing: The Search for a Christian Spirituality*: "Long before we do anything explicitly religious at all, we have to do something about the fire that burns within us. What we do with that fire, how we channel it, is our spirituality" (2014, 7). He goes on to say, "spirituality is about what we do with our souls.... A healthy soul keeps us both energized and glued together" (11–12). This definition notes that spirituality is two things simultaneously: something felt, a passion or a surprising encounter, a gift, which he names as "a fire that burns within us." Spirituality is also a verb: the actions we take to make sense of that feeling, our response to it, and the way we channel it. Our spiritual practices are what we do to integrate that passion in healthy ways. How we respond to the fire within us is the stuff that keeps us "glued together." Rolheiser describes spirituality as both a fire that is completely a gift, and our actions because of it or in response to it keep us glued together. So, hold those two dimensions in mind as we move to explore a couple of other definitions.

Michael Downey also offers a definition of spirituality: "In the most general sense of the term, 'spirituality' refers to the deep desire of the human heart for personal integration in light of levels of reality not immediately apparent, as well as those experiences, events, and efforts which contribute to such integration" (1997, 26). Here again we see a two-pronged definition— the deep desire for integration with something unknown; that noun which is "not immediately apparent" and the verb or action piece, which he describes as "efforts, which contribute to such integration." What both authors point to is that this "fire that burns within us," this "deep desire of the human heart," concerns something beyond ourselves, something we can't quite grasp, yet it demands a response; it requires that we deal with it or channel it through our actions.

I want to point out that both authors are trying to offer a definition of spirituality that is not too quickly tied to one's image of God. They are attempting to get their readers to ponder the depth of feeling they have that is a passion, or a hunger for integration. In the Christian and other monotheistic traditions we would look at the deep feeling, that "fire that burns within us," and name it God. But depending on the context (and the Barnes & Noble employees in upstate New York might agree), the language of spirituality is not limited to talking about God. However, both Rohlheiser and Downey encourage us to recognize that this deep desire—this fire within—comes from something larger than ourselves. Spirituality is a gift and an experience that causes a disconnect or dissonance with our usual normal experiences, and that dissonance motivates activities that "channel it" or make sense of it. The noun is the cause of an experience; the verb is the action taken to unpack that experience.

Mary Frohlich, RSCJ, in her book *Breathed into Wholeness: Catholicity and Life in the Spirit* offers a third definition of spirituality: "Spirituality is a lived experience of the human spirit desiring, seeking, and celebrating communion with what is perceived as worthy of love and self-giving" (2019, 18). Here she notes that once we perceive this reality, this experience of something profoundly new and worthy of our love, we strive for communion with it. When we have a sense of the Spirit, we are willing to give our attention, our focus, and, ultimately, ourselves to it.

So, each of these scholars offer a definition of spirituality that generally starts with the experience of a deep desire or hunger or fire that we perceive within and attempt to make sense of. A noun, an experience, or a gift that comes from beyond our control that we long to relate to and also that demands we grapple with it. One might say spirituality is the encounter with the Spirit, which in turn beckons a response. As Frohlich states, "An experience of the Spirit is not given to a person simply for the sake of having an experience; it is rather an urgent impetus of divine life filling one with energy, vitality and desire to participate in the Spirit's own mission" (2019, 203). Spirituality is the noun that is a gift of the Spirit and also the verb, the way we go about making sense of that gift or urgent impetus. The actions, efforts to channel the lived experience to celebrate and participate in the Spirit's own mission, these are the verbs used to describe the way a spirituality is lived out, and they are what we might call our spiritual practices. So, our two-pronged definition might be summed up as the awareness of and hunger for the Spirit as well as the way we respond to and make sense of that experience in the context of how we live our lives. That whole picture defines spirituality.

Spiritual practices, then, can be understood as any actions we take as an attempt to make sense of how we know and understand our experience of God (or Spirit or something of deep value) and the steps we take that move us toward responding to that experience, toward being in relationship with that fire and attuning our lives to the "urgent impetus" to participate in a vision broader than our own. Our spiritual practices are shaped by, and shape our spirituality in the same way a basketball player is an athlete because of the practices that tone her muscle memory, or a pianist is a musician because of the hours of practice that hone his craft. Our spirituality is shaped by the time and effort we put into attuning our hearts to that thing beyond ourselves we perceive as valuable and worthy of our self-gift.

In the context of faith, attuning our hearts to the rhythm of God's breath shapes our spirituality. Frohlich delves into this image of our spiritual lives patterned on the breathing rhythm of the Spirit. She suggests that, in emptying ourselves, we experience the depth of God within us and then in turn we are sent outward to embrace the fullness of life and our responsibility toward others. "Our spiritual practices are meant to intentionally embody this rhythm of inward and outward movements. . . . The Spirit is the force of infinite love breathing us inward to the apophatic depths of the Father and outward into participation in the Son's salvific action" (2019, 144, 147).

As we explore these definitions of spirituality and spiritual practices, we can begin to see the contours of how theological reflection plays a key role in our life in the Spirit. If we ground our understanding of theological reflection with the presupposition of a sacramental perspective, then we are willing to assume that God is present in our lives. We strive to open our eyes and our hearts to feel the love of God burning within us. Just as the disciples exclaimed after they journeyed on the road to Emmaus, "were not our hearts burning within us as he spoke to us on the way" (Luke 24:32), so too are we encouraged to recognize the movement of the Spirit in the simple conversations we have along the roads of our own lives. This experience of God's love burning within us moves us to actions, and for a Christian to apostolic actions, that pour that love out in solidarity.

The art of theological reflection, as Killen and deBeer would claim, lies in our ability to lay ourselves open to new feelings and insights that bubble to the surface in reflection. Feelings, they note, "are clues to the meaning of our experience. We cannot have transformative insights without them" (1994, 27). Reflection provides the forum for unpacking the feelings of dissonance we feel when we notice injustice or experience oppression or when we have an experience of God's love that challenges us to love deeply in return. Both positive and negative feelings of dissonance motivate us to make changes and respond. Theological reflection as a spiritual practice attends to those feelings and motivations for transformation and carves out the space for the movement of the Spirit. We hear in 1 Corinthians 13, even if I "speak in the tongues of the mortals and the angels, but do not have love, I am a noisy gong or clanging cymbal." The intense feeling of God's love Paul is referring to, or our passion for justice or what Rohlheiser would point to as the "fire that burns within us," must be attended to in reflection. This type of reflective practice grounds our sense of vocation, who we are called to be in the world; without our vocation being grounded in our experience of God's love, we run the risk of simply being noisy cymbals clanging.

DEFINING VOCATION

I have come back time and again throughout my life to this definition of vocation by Fredrick Buechner. One's vocation, he says, "that place God calls you to is where your deep gladness and the world's deep hunger meet" (1973, 118). Each of us has a vocation that both brings us joy and gives our life its meaning. He points out that we are not being asked to do something with our lives that we would despise, but we are asked to consider how we can shape our work as both a joy in our hearts and as a response to the needs of the world. When we stop and reflect on what we are being asked to do in life, we recognize that the choices we make have the ability to impact the wider world. We can respond to the hungers of the world with our passion. In fact, we are most successful and maybe even most helpful when we bring our passion to creatively solve the problems of our piece of the world. Saint Oscar Romero was getting at the same thing in a homily in 1977. He wanted people to realize that every person impacted the world by being holy in the day-in and day-out work that they did.

> How beautiful will be the day when all the baptized understand that their work, their job, is a priestly work, that just as I celebrate Mass at this altar, so each carpenter celebrates Mass at his workbench, and each metal worker, each professional, each doctor with the scalpel, the market woman at her stand, are performing a priestly office! How many cabdrivers, I know, listen to this message in their cabs; you are a priest at the wheel, my friend, if you work with honesty, consecrating that taxi of yours to God, bearing a message of peace and love to the passengers who ride in your cab. (Oscar Romero Homily—November 20, 1977)

One of the realities of life is the need to figure out what we find meaningful, what we are good at, how we can make a living and contribute to something bigger than ourselves. We are all a priestly people, as St. Oscar Romero states. People who figure this out and put themselves at the service of the needs of the world have found their vocation. The very process of figuring this out is theological reflection.

In the context of our vocation, reflection is not only the tool that helps us discern what we are called to do, but also the practice that sustains the work of our vocation over our lifetimes. That metaphor of words spoken without love being just noise is one that cuts close to busy people in ministry. Too often I too have been a noisy cymbal clanging. We can be so bound up in the busyness and needs in front of us that we fail to stop in the moment and reflect on what we are doing and who we are trying to represent to the other. Burnout, anxiety, and stress all build up when we have neglected to hone our reflection skills as a spiritual practice. We find ourselves going through the motions of our regular prayer life or lost in a loop of rumination rather than the reflection that has the rich potential to channel our feelings and draw us closer to God. In these moments we lose a sense of who we are called to be, and our spirituality suffers. Theological reflection is a spiritual practice that not only helps us to glimpse the depths and wholeness of the Spirit, but also helps to shape and define the contours of who we are called to be, and how we are to reflect the Good News into the world. Spirituality and our spiritual practices help to shape and define our vocation or our understanding of how the work of our hands matches the depths of our love.

I point out these definitions of vocation and spirituality to lift up a common thread in both aspects of our lives: reflection is critical to both. We have to spend time reflecting on what we are passionate about and what brings us joy. We need to reflect on where the world is hurting, and how we might respond. We need to reflect when embarking on life-integration and transformation—those things do not happen without reflection. Reflection carves out the space to examine our actions and the world around us and to discern a response. Reflection is a critical key to a life well lived. Even Socrates stated, in Plato's *Apology*, "The unexamined life is not worth living." And my colleague Ed Foley drew on this quote to remark, "unexamined faith is not sustainable." Reflection and, in the context of a faith tradition, theological reflection becomes the tool necessary to sustain and shape spirituality.

SPIRITUAL PRACTICES

Reflection is a vital spiritual practice. Many of the most celebrated spiritual masters give evidence of the time they spend in reflective practice. Frohlich names a pattern evident in the writings of spiritual giants such as Julian of Norwich when she notes: "A sequence of experience of God, followed by a period of rumination on the memory (or memories), eventually bearing fruit in theological elaboration, may be the unacknowledged root of all authentic theological insight" (2019, 186–187). What she notes as the "period of rumination, which bears fruit" is, I would claim, theological reflection. The key is to develop the skills of reflective practice so that our spiritual lives are shaped and challenged to grow. Reflection bears fruit in the context of a community that values participation in a vision of solidarity and hope. Spiritual practices need the integration that is a byproduct of reflection in order to bear fruit, and theological reflection itself is a process and practice that cultivates spiritual growth.

Theological reflection not only creates the space to reflect on experiences of God and what that means for the future, but also affords the opportunity to reflect further back in time on past experiences which seemed unremarkable to mine them for glimpses of God we may have missed the first time around. If we truly believe in the sacramental principle, that God is present in all things, then we must challenge ourselves to notice the extraordinary in the mundane regularly. To "see with eyes that can see!" If we reflect on the ordinary moments of life and trust that God is present in them, our reflection bears fruit in our growing spirituality.

St. Ignatius of Loyola developed the *Spiritual Exercises*, a thirty-day retreat that invites the participants through a series of themes that cultivate a heart that can see God in all things and helps them reorder their lives in accord with God's movements. For Ignatius, the imaginative starting point is to examine a story from the life of Jesus. By contemplating a story from scripture, (an example could be the story of Jesus at the tomb of Lazarus), participants are invited to a deep reflection that allows them to experience the story in new and revelatory ways. One might contemplate the feelings of loss of Martha and Mary, what Lazarus' sisters, felt, the curiosity of the crowd gathered around the tomb, or even Lazarus' confusion or amazement as he emerged into new life. In putting oneself in the shoes of someone in the scene, we explore the spiritual wisdom that comes from aligning our lives with the story of our faith. The insights drawn from this type of reflection have much depth. The Ignatian move to *imagine one's self in Jesus' story* is one way to see God in all things. In theological reflection, we can also turn *to imagine God in our own story*. By trusting the sacramental principal, that in fact all of life is permeated with the Spirit, theological reflection as a spiritual practice presents the opportunity to carve out the space to recognize the rhythms of God in any moment of our lives. Beyond personal reflection, theological reflection also engages a community in shared spiritual practice.

In addition to reflecting on experiences of God, theological reflection as a spiritual practice also creates opportunities to see God in new ways. In carving out this sacred space to catch glimpses of God, the time we spend in theological reflection itself becomes a sacred space for spiritual experiences. The ability to enter into conversation with others in an environment of respect and trust that encourages a willingness to be "parabled" by God is indeed a spiritual experience and practice that shapes and reshapes us. As Frohlich notes, the vulnerability it takes to open up to God's perspective of us can be tough. "The way of emptying deconstructs us, unveiling our brokenness, incompleteness, and ultimate vulnerability—and, in the same movement, revealing that these fissures are the very place where the Spirit rushes in to embrace us in tenderest communion" (2019, 218). In this vulnerability, we recognize we can be renewed and transformed. The reflective pattern to pause and pay attention, to seek God's nearness, and engage in transformation, is a spiritual practice that has shaped venerated saints such as Julian of Norwich, St. Ignatius of Loyola, and everyday saints such as you and me.

DIALOGUE AS SPIRITUAL PRACTICE

Another avenue that I would like to explore in looking at theological reflection as a spiritual practice is the notion of dialogue. Our look at the two saints above spoke of spiritual practices that were individual journeys; I assert that dialogue is an important piece of the spiritual practice of theological reflection, especially through the lens of parables. As Crossan said, "it takes two to parable!" The communal aspect of theological reflection is imperative and holds depth of meaning. The story about developing our family brand that I noted at the beginning of this chapter began with an experience of dissonance and moved to a dialogue as a family. Likewise, the period of theological reflection is rich when we explore together the movement of the Spirit. We will first look at the spiritual practice of contemplative dialogue and then the practice of *prophetic dialogue* as developed by Steve Bevans, SVD, and Roger Schroeder, SVD. Each reveals the importance of dialogue as a spiritual practice that cultivates the heart for transformation.

Contemplative dialogue is considered a group spiritual practice that encourages participants to have a contemplative stance toward one another and toward their context in an effort to enter into dialogue that is insightful and fruitful. "The general pattern is a process in which a group seeks to access together a deep interior contemplative space and then to dialogue toward discovery of the group actions that arise from this collective awareness" (Frohlich 2019, 219). This pattern, which begins with dialogue and moves toward group action, is considered a spiritual practice because of its focus on contemplation and the inherent connection with contemplating God's perspective. The Leadership Council of Women Religious developed a video: *Contemplative Dialogue: Unleashing the Transformative Power of Communal Wisdom* (lcwr.org/contemplative-dialogue). This video showcases a process of contemplative dialogue aimed at cultivating space for communal transformation. As Frohlich notes, "This practice, then, enables individuals and groups to grow in their capacity to work collectively to build relationships, solve problems and enhance the common good" (2019, 219). Contemplative dialogue, like theological reflection at its best, is a communal effort to respond to an experience of God's nearness, and that response is one that brings about Good News. When we enter into dialogue that is a conscious attempt to put ourselves in the presence of God, we cannot help but be challenged by a perspective on the ways we could change or grow in being Good News for the world around us.

The practice of dialogue that leads to Good News is also at the heart of prophetic dialogue as defined by Bevans and Schroeder.[1] I would like to point, particularly, to how they define prophetic dialogue and where their discussion intersects with how we consider theological reflection as a spiritual practice.

The phrase, *Prophetic Dialogue*, began to be used in the discussions of the Society of Divine Word Missionaries 15th General Chapter in 2000. The idea has been developed since in the context of their SVD missionary work. The suggestion is that missionaries start with a stance of dialogue that invites them to be humbly open to the perspective of the "other." This stance includes a dimension that is prophetic, that encourages both dialogue partners to be open to the perspective of the "other," and how that might offer a critique or challenge. They encourage that one "approaches the 'other' with an initial attitude of discerning how God is already present (dialogue) and then eventually, together *with* the people, after developing respect and mutual relationships, confronts the 'weeds' with the 'Good News' (prophecy)" (Bevans and Schroeder 2011, 75). I will note here that they are clear that prophetic dialogue has the potential to point out the "weeds" in both participants in the dialogue; the heart of prophetic dialogue lies in the humility necessary to build trust and foster growth in all parties. The stance of vulnerability allows for a commitment to being "together *with* the people" in a way that transforms the whole. Schroeder and Bevans see the work of prophetic dialogue functioning "more as a spirituality than a strategy" in their missionary work (2011, 2).

Prophetic dialogue has both the noun and verb dimensions of spirituality that we pointed out in our earlier definitions. The noun dimension is the one that glimpses God already present in the other and the verb is the movement outward toward transformation that happens when the shared dialogue exposes a prophetic way forward. Just as with the sacramental presupposition of theological reflection, prophetic dialogue begins with the conviction that God is already there and that, through dialogue and the risk of vulnerability, not only can we encounter God's surprising nearness, but we also lay ourselves open to discerning the "weeds" that persist. Both prophetic dialogue and theological reflection privilege the awareness of God's nearness in the "other," and the regular encounters in life have a parabolic or prophetic impulse moving participants to transformation.

Contemplative dialogue and prophetic dialogue both offer frameworks for how dialogue becomes a spiritual practice and at times even a spiritual experience. Both suggest that the move to communion in dialogue is the starting point for transformative actions that bear fruit in the relationships and life of people. Cochrane argues for a move beyond dialogue to intentionally listen for the voices of those at the margins because their perspective is critical to the whole community of faith. "A commitment to perspectives on the margins of society, away from the centers of power and wealth, becomes fundamental to the theological enterprise" (Cochrane 1999, 151). And as we noted earlier in chapter 4, he further differentiates between simply listening and truly attempting to understand their perspectives. "To do so means distinguishing between conversation (dialogue) and collaboration (solidarity). Collaboration takes the form of commitment to a partner who may not be equal in respect or access to and use of power" (Cochrane 1999, 169).

THEOLOGICAL REFLECTION THROUGH THE LENS OF PARABLES AS SPIRITUAL PRACTICE

This move from dialogue to solidarity is evident in prophetic dialogue and a critical outcome of theological reflection through the lens of parables. As Cochrane notes, the movement is from conversation to collaboration. More than simply sharing stories and getting to know each other, theological reflection is a spiritual practice that opens up avenues for exposure and critique, challenge and transformation. As we have noted, theological reflection is a collaborative effort to discern God's presence in the world and respond in ways that promote participation in God's Good News. Thus, our theological reflection becomes a spiritual practice that shapes not only our spirituality but also our vocation. Through theological reflection we are in touch with how we respond with our lives to the cries of the world. I would argue that, in fact, spirituality and spiritual practices that do not move us to this type of prophetic collaboration are incomplete; we have not yet pushed them to the deepest actions possible. The move from dialogue to solidarity aligns our lives with God's prophetic action in the world. Through theological reflection we not only feel more clearly the "fire that burns within us," but we also carve the space and take the steps that channel that fire in ways that enter into collaborative relationships for the common good of all.

This move to prophetic collaboration and transformative solidarity is a critical piece of theological reflection in parabolic mode. When we ask, "What does solidarity have to do with theological reflection?" the lens of parables keeps narrowing the focus of theological reflection to the question of solidarity and authentically living our lives in the Spirit. What role does theological reflection have to play, whether we stand at the margins or in contexts of relative privilege, in challenging us to consider solidarity with each other as vital to our spirituality? How does theological reflection provide the space to adequately look at and learn from experiences of dissonance?

This willingness to have our "tidy vision of reality shattered" is at the heart of what it means to be "parabled" as Crossan claims. To be exposed through the communal dialogue of theological reflection to the perspective of who we are before God and what we can be shapes our spirituality and our vocation. As Frohlich noted earlier, these very places of being shattered are where "the Spirit rushes in in tenderest communion." Solidarity with one another and in the presence of the Spirit is an example of this tender communion. Solidarity and the prerequisites of trust and respect in dialogue are the fruits of parabolic theological reflection as a spiritual practice.

I gave the example at the beginning of this chapter of my family and our conversation around family brands. This was hardly a deep reflection on solidarity, but the steps of that process are still evident. The feelings of dissonance that my husband and I felt were a form of listening to the voices of children and the negative impact branding and marketing had on their psyches. Our stance of protection and response came from a position of solidarity within our family, but rather than make sweeping decisions from our position of power as parents, we engaged in a dialogue with our children to allow them to privilege their own voices and name their own value symbols. The actions we took, together as a family, were more authentic because of that shared conversation and had an impact that resulted in a habit of Good News over time. The ripple effects of that conversation and the subsequent actions are hard to trace with straight lines, but there is no doubt they have surfaced throughout life in subtle ways. Again, this was hardly a deep reflection about solidarity, but it gives us a starting example of how dialogue and reflection are intertwined with spirituality and vocation.

A more pressing example might be to consider those whose life work involves peacebuilding and how they are shaped by their reflection and moral imagination. John Paul Lederach gave a talk to the Association of Conflict Resolution in 2004 titled: *The Moral Imagination: The Art and Soul of Building Peace*.[2] In this address he poignantly discusses moral imagination and the critical elements necessary to sustain a life of peacebuilding. He defines moral imagination as "the wellspring that is rooted in the challenges of the real world yet is capable of giving birth to that which does not yet exist" (2007, 16). His definition ties in closely with a sense of spirituality that is rooted in the experiences of life and yet in touch with the possibilities for transformation. His "wellspring" is a passion for the other like Rolheiser's "fire that burns within," and the verb of spirituality is akin to the actions that are yet to be birthed. Moral imagination in the context of peacebuilding, it would seem, is the sacred space that cultivates the actions of a rich spirituality. Moral imagination is a spiritual practice just as prophetic dialogue or theological reflection.

In his address, Lederach names what he sees as four critical elements to the art of peacebuilding. I will include a brief description of each element as they each hold dramatic similarity to elements of spirituality and the spiritual practice of theological reflection. First, he notes the art of being in relationship. "The artistic process has this dialectic nature: It rises from human experience, then shapes, gives expression and meaning to that experience . . . who we have been, are and will be emerges and shapes itself in a context of relational interdependency." Notice his focus on the dialogue and the relationships with those who shape and give meaning to our lives. This relational interdependency is on par with solidarity, and the impetus for meaning that is bound up with one another.

Next he discusses curiosity: a curiosity that longs to learn from and stay attentive to the other and that breeds a deep level of care that ignites a passion for the other. "Curiosity is about passion: A passion for people, for Truth, for meaning, for healing, for constructive change" (2007, 17). Here we see the similarity between Lederach's curiosity and theological reflections' parabolic commitment to standing in solidarity with those at the margins. It takes a curiosity to get to know the other, to do a deep dive into the context of their lives, and to share from the depth of our own lives as well. This depth of curiosity that moves toward solidarity reflects the passion necessary to move toward healing and a transformative change. It begins with those we encounter in relationship and dialogue and is lived out in collaboration for a future yet unknown.

The third element Lederach names as necessary for moral imagination is creativity: "I believe that the primary role of the moral imagination is to provide space for the creative act to emerge. Providing space requires a predisposition, a kind of attitude and perspective that opens up, even invokes the spirit and belief that creativity is humanly possible" (2007, 18). He then goes on to note that acts of creativity "give rise to the unexpected." This unexpected, or as I would suggest this parabolic surprise, is the hope and belief that things can change. Note his conviction that creativity is cultivated in multiple spaces—the physical space of pausing to reflect and allow creative acts to emerge, but also the cultivated space in a heart open to invoking the Spirit's surprising perspective.

The fourth and final element that Lederach notes as critical to peacebuilding is risk. The risk it takes to step into those spaces in need of peacebuilding is paradoxical because our lives become entangled or intertwined with those whose lives are turned upside down by violence and the risks they take to step into hope. In either case, the risks taken require the stance of vulnerability that is important for theological reflection. "Risk by its very nature is mysterious. It is mystery lived, for it ventures into lands that are not controlled or charted" (2007, 18). Lederach's expectation that relationship, curiosity, creativity, and risk hold the keys to cultivating a moral imagination are in line with our own development of theological reflection as a spiritual practice: a communal effort, a web of relationships built on trust, respect, and mutual engagement. These relationships are sustained in dialogue by the stories we tell not only to get to know one another but also to find common values and dreams for the future. The process of theological reflection opens up space for both creativity and vulnerability. We venture into these uncharted waters and there find surprising glimpses of God in solidarity with us. In the sacred space of theological reflection these glimpses of God, or these moments of solidarity, move us with passion to embody acts of courage, love, and hope which in turn transform the world.

The experience of God's love, or passion for justice, or the fire that burns within us is a dissonance that compels us toward change. Peacebuilders set about their work because of a sense of dissonance and longing for peace. Their curiosity and creativity become the dialogue of theological reflection that encourages them to risk security for a vision of peace that in turn becomes a habitus of peacebuilding. Lederach's presentation of the moral imagination is a lifelong theological reflection engaged at the peripheries of power and in solidarity with people and communities across the world working for peace and conflict resolution. He shares a multitude of stories from his life experiences as a way to carry the stories and voices of those who have shaped him and others committed to peacebuilding. He carries these stories into what he teaches and shares with others in his network of relationships. His passion and the passion of those who share his craft are fueled by a glimpse of what is possible when curiosity, creativity, and risks are shared in communion with others longing for a common good of justice and solidarity. These acts of peacebuilding are sustained by the moral imagination that claims its reflective space in the hearts and minds of those willing to risk aligning their spirituality and passion with the cries of others.

What I have tried to trace my finger over in this chapter is a conviction that theological reflection is a spiritual practice available to any person or group of people who wish to gain perspective and push their sense of who they are called to be in light of their experience of the Spirit. Exploring theological reflection through the lens of parables offers a provocative frame for not only reflecting on the experiences of life, but also of opening ourselves up to the shocking challenge to recognize God in the world and align our hearts and our vocation with God's message of hope and love. Theological reflection is a spiritual practice that helps us to tell our story in light of this fire that burns within us and imagine the possibilities that could arise when our story becomes our story of faith.

Schillebeeckx talks of writing a fifth Gospel with our lives. "In the end we have here the convergence of two stories, the story of the Gospel tradition of faith and the story of our personal and social life which in the best instances has itself as it were become 'gospel' a fifth or umpteenth gospel" (Schilleebeckx, *Church*, 34). Perhaps as we take up Schillebeeckx's challenge, we might find that we too are challenged to live lives that are parabolic. Earlier we discussed how a parable assumes a storyteller and a listener that are two distinct entities—that parables surprise their listener. If we are now telling the parable, then let us tell it in a way that surprises God back.

NOTES

1. For a fuller description of prophetic dialogue, please see their book, *Prophetic Dialogue: Reflections on Christian Mission Today* (Maryknoll, 2011).

2. The full transcript of John Paul Lederach's talk was published in the Autumn 2007 issue of *European Judaism* (Vol 40, No 2, 2007, 1–21).

Chapter 6

Practicing Reflection
Reflective Practice through the Lens of Parables

The first five chapters of this project have laid the groundwork for the reader to not only become a reflective practitioner, but also one open to the critique of being parabled. Tying the simple stories of my children into the framework of each chapter was an effort to point out that everyone, regardless of age or education, could build up the habit of reflection as a spiritual practice. Our life has much more depth when we pause and reflect, gather with one another, and open ourselves up to new perspectives of hope.

I shared the stories of my students and my ministerial experiences throughout with the hopes of inviting those of you who are ministers not only to build the habit of reflection, but also to take seriously the task of *theological* reflection. People in ministry have the critical task of helping others make "faith-sense" of the everyday. Our success as a minister lies in our ability to cultivate a sacramental perspective in our own hearts as well as in the hearts of those with whom we minister. Theological reflection builds our capacity for noticing God in the world and for wrestling with the invitation to transformation such reflection unpacks. Transformation is an integral part of what it means to be people of faith; a community that is open to growth will always be open to God's surprising nearness and find its foundation in justice. Theological reflection grounded in the simple pattern of parables taps the depths of the mission and ministry of Jesus. He shared simple stories that had profound implications of justice and mercy. If theological reflection is to have a lasting impact on our lives and ministry, we too must be open to having our vision and our expectations turned upside down. Theological reflection that guides a community of faith to *metanoia* is a spiritual practice that leads to solidarity and hope. This is our task—to be people of hope, people of Good News. Theological reflection through the lens of parables is a tool that shapes and forms us into a people of hope, bound up with the least of our brothers and sisters, and open to the surprising nearness of God.

REVISITING THE DEFINITION

It might be helpful to revisit the definition of theological reflection presented in the second chapter: theological reflection at its best is a communal effort to discern God's presence in the world, to carve the space for that presence to invite us into a new vision and to lay the groundwork for that new vision to take root in how we live our lives. This definition was evident as we explored the role of parables in theological reflection. Theological reflection through the lens of parables is the effort to carve out a sacred space to pause and consider the familiar experiences of everyday life from new angles, to notice the movement of the Spirit in the surprising moments that challenge us to a new vision, and to allow that new vision to invite us to shape lives rooted in justice and solidarity.

If we were to place theological reflection through the lens of parables on the taxonomy developed by Kinast in his book *What are they saying about Theological Reflection*, we might recognize that each of the categories can be considered through the lens of parables. This lens provides an overlapping framework for the task of ministerial theological reflection by refocusing the discussion not only on the ministry incidents and how ministers can respond differently in the future, but also on how they recognize God's subversive presence in their work and in the people with whom they minister. Theological reflection through the lens of parables can also be seen as a spiritual practice situated within the category of spiritual wisdom styles of reflection. As Kinast notes, the spiritual style of theological reflection fosters "the wisdom proper to the life of the believer" (2000, 16), and theological reflection through the lens of parables offers an accessible yet provocative way to cultivate the spiritual lives of people of faith.

Although this lens was formed initially with the Christian tradition of parables in mind, the possibilities for adaptation with different traditions and cultures is made possible by the vulnerability required to create sacred spaces of *metanoia*. There are parables in the Qur'an and parabolic sayings in the Hebrew scriptures as well as other religious traditions. Leaders of multifaith groups invite participants to tap their own sacred texts for the surprising invitations to transformation, thus encouraging interreligious dialogue as well. Encouraging interreligious and intercultural dialogue through the lens of parables draws on the vulnerability and openness necessary to be parabled by the other.

The lens of parable also has practical implications in line with the practical style of theological reflection by its focus on parabolic transformation as the invitation to stand with those on the margins. Such a stance *presumes* a praxis grounded in the life and needs of a community and its context, with a stance of humility and mutual respect. The liberative lens of feminist theological reflection has also influenced the development and implementation of parabolic theological reflection. Claiming that experiences of any person, no matter their gender, age, or education level, and celebrating the stories of children, our earth, and other vulnerable populations as Good Nûews are all critical components of the parabolic methodology as a liberative lens.

The lens of parables can be layered over other methods of theological reflection to provide a framework for progression and a focus on the transformative power of reflective practice. Theological reflection is one of the most important tools in the ministerial toolbox, and the lens of parables aids in the adaptation and creative expression of reflective practice for a wide diversity of contexts. The remainder of this chapter will highlight a number of areas for this adaptation and creativity. It steps into the waters of practice by providing variations on reflection adapted to multiple different settings. This section is designed to encourage reflection and reflective practice and, specifically, to hone the skill and habit of reflection through the lens of parables.

PRACTICE, PRACTICE, PRACTICE

In Relationships

As has been mentioned throughout, it is critical that people who participate in theological reflection have a sense of their own contextual lenses. Knowing how one's own culture, faith tradition, age, or gender (among other things) influences the way we see the world and respond is a significant part of the reflective process. It helps to know the contextual lenses each participant operates out of as we begin to consider adapting parable as a lens for reflection. The first place that we begin to adapt our reflective practice is as a person in relationship with other people. Reflective practice happens in life as we engage in relationships and communicate and respond to others. The lens of parables fosters growth and dialogue between spouses, parents and children, siblings and extended family, and so on. Even our relationships with friends, acquaintances, and coworkers are all impacted by our ability to be reflective of the contours of these relationships. Think of an encounter you have had recently with someone in your close circle of friends and family. Can you unpack it with the three-question formula of the lens of parables? "What is familiar, what is surprising, and how is that an invitation to Good News?" This type of reflective practice reminds us to pause in the midst of life to consider how our relationships are a reflection of the presence of God in the world. I am one of eight children in my family, and even in our forties and fifties there are times I just have to smile as the familiar patterns of relating become our default methods of communication. But every once in a while, a conversation or a discussion involving care of our parents or holiday planning will surprise me. Someone will have a response that was unexpected, and without skipping a beat the discussion takes a new path forward. I find myself trying to pay closer attention in the moment, to name the surprising responses and explore together how that shift was an invitation to move in a positive direction. The parabolic framework has me not only noticing surprising breakthroughs, but also checking my own assumptions of what is familiar and how I have limited the paths forward. When we talk about these types of observations as family, we realize that we grow and shift in relationships, and that the familiar patterns have changed, too. Naming that shifting and growing is an intentional way of celebrating the hope that flows from relationships of trust and love.

The ability to utilize the parabolic lens as a reflective tool in the midst of relationships is something that works in ministerial or work settings, too. Once I was having a particularly intense conversation with the DRE at my parish. I was a parent of children in the school, and my oldest was preparing for First Communion. I had suggested a service project as a way to not only involve the families in the life of the parish but also as a way to encourage the students to understand what it meant to "shine Christ's light" into the world. We had very different assumptions about the capacity of the first communicants and their families to engage in the suggested day of service. While she was frustrated with the families that do not come to church regularly and their lack of interest in anything more than the bare minimum of requirements, I pushed back reminding her that I was a second-grade parent too and wanted to get involved. In our conversation, we agreed that we were both familiar with her concerns that families are hard to engage in the life of the parish. But we also agreed that the effort might be something other than their usual expectations and perhaps would hit a different chord. In the end, she agreed to allow me to "give it a try," and we were both surprised by the 95 percent participation of the first communicants and their families. As I reflected on the conversation and the relationship between the two of us, I know it took a lot for her to meet me in the middle on this one, and that, too, was enough of a surprise for me to keep building on the relationship as we continued to work together on different projects.

In Parish or Congregational Ministry

The task of theological reflection through the lens of parables is a helpful tool in relationship building, but the crux of this tool comes into play in the adaptations for multiple group settings from ministry, to education, to workplace planning. In ministry settings, any committee, council, staff, or planning meeting can include theological reflection as a regular part of the meeting agenda. Some parishes build time for reflective conversation into meeting agendas on a regular basis, while others utilize theological reflection as they plan and discern major decisions. One example of such a parish theological reflection is the community attempting to discern whether or not they would allow the various organizations of the parish to hold fundraisers in the church vestibule after masses. The new pastor was a bit turned off by the chaos and saw the selling of items reminiscent of the money changers in the temple that irked Jesus in his day. Rather than make a unilateral decision, though, he asked the parish council to help. They in turn decided to engage the parish community in a theological reflection around the question. They began by asking various groups within the community for feedback, putting survey cards in the pews, with a priority on gathering feedback from those who attended daily or Sunday masses regularly. The first question asked was, "What do you notice when groups sell cookies or popcorn or flowers in the vestibule?" The second question was "What scripture story comes to mind when you notice this type of activity?" When the pastor and the parish council sat down to read the responses, they were surprised. Overwhelmingly the community noted that the flurry of activity and color in the vestibule after masses was delightful and joyful. Elderly members noted that they looked forward to seeing the children, to supporting their causes, and to enjoying the treasures of Girl Scout cookies or flowers back in the quiet of their own homes. They felt such items connected them to the whole community. Younger parents noted that they were always touched by the interactions with the older parishioners who always seemed to be so supportive and willing to share a story from when they were a Girl Scout or when they had kids in the school. The scriptures that were noted were phrases such as "let the little children come to me" or "Jesus as a child in the temple." The only scripture that mentioned money was "the widow's mite" referenced by one woman who said she felt like the widow giving so very little, but she was glad to be able to share it with the children. The conversation was fruitful, and the decision was an easy one. Even the pastor saw the flurry of activity with new eyes, realizing the relationships it fostered and the joy it brought to the wider community.

Parish finance councils are also places where this type of parabolic theological reflection can play an important role. Often, finance meetings tend to be focused on money and budgets and lack a connection to the overall mission of the faith community. By developing a pattern of engaging stories from the community at the start of each meeting, or through a retreat day at the beginning of the year, the participants build their sense of mission and vision that frames the budget work as an integral part of that mission. When this type of mission integration happens, finance councils move from entities focused on stretching limited funds to ones empowered to collaborate in God's surprising miracles of abundance. Just as in the story above, being able to see situations with fresh perspectives helps break open surprising ways forward.

Another example of adapting theological reflection in the parabolic mode in a congregational setting is when a church utilized it as a tool for reflection at a volunteer appreciation evening. The group gathered consisted of members of the community who were lectors, greeters, ushers, choir members, and Eucharistic ministers. They were encouraged to reflect together on what it meant to give of themselves to the liturgical celebration of the community. When asked what was familiar about their service, people commented how they enjoyed seeing the familiar faces of community members as they walk in the doors or up for communion or of feeling that they wish they could do more, but at least this was what they could offer. They also hoped that they shared the hospitality of their community with others.

As they discussed the pieces that felt familiar, they were encouraged to consider any scripture stories that came to mind. They talked about the woman anointing Jesus with her hair and how Jesus responded saying "She has done what she could." That felt empowering to them, because although they cannot do everything the parish needs, they can step up and do a little. Other scriptures that came to mind were stories when Jesus called his disciples to follow him. Specific groups, like the choir, recounted musical themes such as "even the stones will sing out in praise," and Eucharistic ministers thought of the last supper and Jesus washing the feet of his disciples. Each of these stories provided more ways to connect their experiences of volunteering in the community to the stories of Jesus' ministry in the world, and their ministry felt empowering.

When asked what surprised them, there was a rich discussion about how they oftentimes feel when they see the same people doing all the work, but when they looked around the room at one another, they realized there were far more people involved than they normally assumed. They were also surprised that each of the scripture passages that were discussed seemed to shed light on the value of their role in the community. What became apparent was that, although the pastoral staff had organized the day to say thank you, what ended up being the main thrust of the day was for the volunteers themselves to value and appreciate all they bring to the community and to value and appreciate one another. If the pastoral staff had simply designed a prayer service of appreciation, without providing the volunteers an opportunity to step into the discussion and explore their own feelings, this would have been a missed opportunity. Instead, the staff was able to watch as the volunteers leaned into understanding the importance of their contribution to the community. By giving the volunteers a chance to be a part of the dialogue at the event, they opened up an avenue that allowed the volunteers to appreciate their contributions as a part of their own vocation within the community. The renewed sense of involvement that came from this shared reflective appreciation night was transformative for the volunteers and the pastoral staff too.

Educational Settings

Theological reflection plays a critical role in the education of ministers. James and Evelyn Whitehead's *Method in Ministry* set the stage for ministerial students to engage in the practice of theological reflection as a way to integrate their theological studies with the work they did in the midst of a community of faith. The next adaptation called for is to move this type of pedagogy into the realm of distance learning. More and more degree programs are completed entirely online, and this calls for a creative adaptation of theological reflection into a digital classroom. At Catholic Theological Union this happens in three different ways. First, we simply move the small-group conversations to a Zoom or Google classroom format where the group gathers just as it would in a face-to-face classroom. Our distance learning students appreciate the opportunity to meet their classmates in a virtual face-to-face space, and during the COVID-19 pandemic, even our in-person classrooms were quickly shifted to Zoom formats, and the students felt that they did not skip a beat in terms of the depth of their discussions. We have also adapted theological reflection for a one-to-one conversation over the course of a year for students involved in immersion ministry experiences. Students are asked to write up an in-depth theological reflection each month of their ministry immersion, and they receive feedback from their faculty in the form of an ongoing conversation. Although this is not a group setting, the two-person conversations do lead to fruitful reflections. Just as importantly, it requires students to carve out the space for reflection, which helps to develop the habit of reflective practice as they navigate full-time ministry.

In addition, we adapt for asynchronized theological reflection. Our students come from many different continents and time zones, and the need to coordinate learning to central standard time feels a bit hegemonic. As a response, a discussion forum is set up on our digital classroom platform and arranged for small groups of students to respond to one another online, each discussion taking place over the span of a week. Each student logs into the discussion when it works best during their own time zone. On day one, a designated student shares a video in which they talk about a particular ministerial incident. By day three, all students (and their faculty facilitator) respond with posts naming what they see as familiar, what sources they draw from when exploring the familiar pieces of this story, and what they find as surprising or challenging. In the interim days they are encouraged to read the responses of their peers and keep the conversation flowing. By day five, students share insights they have gleaned from reading all of the discussion points thus far and what they perceive as the invitation from the points of surprise. The student who brought the initial story to the group participates in all aspects of the discussion forum and shares insights that they gained from the group's wisdom process. The final piece of the discussion forum is for all of the students to name ways these insights could result in their own transformation or Good News for those on the margins. A week-long conversation with three students and one faculty participant results in about 20–30 posts and responses per week, and students have expressed appreciation for the ability to do this in an asynchronized setting. Students who have experienced both face-to-face and asynchronized theological reflection small groups have noted that they find both settings can offer provocative insights and challenges to their ministry. These are three different ways of adapting theological reflection for ministerial education in the era of online learning. Theological reflection, however, is not limited to theology students or ministerial training. There are plenty of opportunities for adaptation into other educational settings as well.

High schools or colleges often utilize theological reflection as a tool for the integrative work of their service-learning curriculum. Engaging students with reflective practices that help them connect their service activities with their sense of who they could become is a formative process. The time spent in reflection is critical, and carving out the space for reflection in the planning stages helps to set the tone that this integrative work is just as important as the service itself. There are a number of possibilities for such planning at the high school level.

In some cases, schools have a requirement that students engage in service but their projects are organized at assorted times and there is no arranged time within a class for the integrative work of reflection. In these situations, the persons in charge of making sure students do this service work often scramble for ways to help students make sense of this requirement. One suggestion is to develop a *Service Journal* for students to complete once they have participated in a service activity. Appendix B has one example of a *Service Journal* designed for a public high school. Schools that are free to include their language of faith can add additional questions along those lines. In one particular setting, the school chose to print their *Service Journals* on two ply carbonless papers. This allowed students to turn in the top copy in and keep a copy for themselves. The students were required to turn in one journal for each of four required service projects and at the end of the year they met one on one with their service-learning coordinator to talk about all four projects and journal submissions.

When a school allows the opportunity to utilize class time for the integrative work of service learning, activities that prepare students for service experiences can take place in classes leading up to the volunteer service. The "what is familiar?" stage can be developed over time as students learn about a particular issue or community in their classes—and not just theology classes. Depending on the focus of the service, English classes can assign students to pay attention to how their issue is portrayed in the news, math classes can look at statistical information on the neighborhood, or science classes can consider what environmental questions might come into play. Based on the type of project planned, engaging in social analysis, introducing concepts of Catholic social teaching, or assigning students to prepare "thick descriptions" of the context can be done ahead of time as part of the curriculum leading up to or alongside service experiences. All of this becomes the part of the reflection that asks, "What is familiar?" Teachers appreciate being provided with the resources and information necessary to build this into the curriculum. If possible, collaborative working teams can develop these resources and encourage participation. This effort helps students realize that service is a part of the culture of the school, not simply an extracurricular.

If a whole grade or class is able to do a one-day service project, then there are more opportunities for reflective work. Conversations on the bus rides to and from, during the lunch breaks, or in the midst of the work itself are all opportunities for the students to learn to pay attention to the possibilities of Grace. On the bus ride over, encourage students to pay attention to what they see, hear, smell, touch, and taste during their service experiences. The familiarity of using their senses not only helps them to remember more details of the events, but also invites them to consider the lenses through which they experience the moment. They can also be engaged in conversations about their hopes or fears leading into the day. On the bus ride home, give students an opportunity to share one word or image from the day that caused them to pause and reflect. Questions that invite them to share what surprised them, shocked them, or made them feel uncomfortable are questions that high school students engage easily. They will quickly offer a point of critique of things that they didn't like or things that made them uncomfortable. It is often easy for them to find something that stuck out to them, and others will respond in kind.

If facilitated well, their engagement with what surprised them leads to new perspectives. Taking the time to trace for them the line between what surprised them and how that might be an invitation for them to see God's nearness or participate in the Good News is the next step of theological reflection. Students who were uncomfortable with the way someone smelled might be encouraged to reflect on the gift of a shower and whether or not they take that for granted. Students might note their own discomfort when someone spoke a different language or was elderly or in some other way different from their own life experience. The teacher, campus minister, or parent's ability to facilitate the conversation to discuss prejudice or difference in an invitational stance is critical. If a student was surprised by how much litter they picked up on the beach, they might be encouraged to consider their own use of single-use plastics or to examine the ways garbage is discarded from their own homes. Service-learning projects are not geared to change the whole world, but to change the worldviews of the student participants. The impact of a single service project on the community is minimal if we are counting hours spent or work completed. But if we have done a good job of creating sacred spaces, then the ground cultivated for transformative growth in the minds and hearts of future leaders has an impact that is far greater.

In addition to service-learning settings, educational pedagogy can creatively adapt theological reflection to dig deeply into topics covered in the curriculum. At one point I was designing a way to educate high school students about Pope Francis' encyclical on the environment, *Laudato Sí*. The goal was to build up their passion around environmental issues and their capacity for activism. In the midst of our discussions about caring for creation and the impact high school students might have on the wider society's commitment to making change, I showed them a Calvin and Hobbes comic strip from July 30, 1988. (see figure 6.1)

I asked the students to look at the comic strip and name what was familiar there. They first enjoyed the familiarity of Calvin and his usual antics of power and control. But when pushed to consider who or what they identified with, they started pondering several different insights. They noted that they felt like the flowers—unable to get the person with power to share anything they needed. They were familiar with the thought of leaders making choices not for a common good, but just on a whim, and maybe even on mean streak. They were also familiar with the thought that the flowers were thirsty and felt a desire to protect our parched earth. Some of the students said they felt like the water in the watering can—they knew what the flowers needed but were too small to get there on their own and a bigger power was keeping them away. Some students also thought that perhaps they were familiar with the

Figure 6.1 **Calvin and Hobbes.** *Source*: © 1988 Watterson. Reprinted with permission of ANDREWS MCMEEL SYNDICATION. All rights reserved.

sense that Calvin really didn't understand what he was saying. He might think he holds the flowers' lives in his hands, but does he really, and does he really want them to die? They also felt the familiar joy of a cool rain on a hot day, and the refreshment of a cool drink of water.

Next I asked the students to name what surprised them here. The first surprise they shared was the rain that covered the final square. That felt refreshing and unexpected, a pure gift. They also were surprised at how they felt relieved when the rain fell just as much to refresh the flowers as to refresh Calvin and his limited supply of water in the watering can. Their discussion took a compassionate turn for those in power who might miss their own connectedness and dependency on the rain. Those students that had identified with the water in the watering can felt surprisingly empowered. They realized that even though their efforts were (in this comic strip literally) a drop in the bucket, they were not alone. All those who are marginalized and nature itself welled up and nourished everyone in ways they had not anticipated at the beginning. As you can begin to surmise from the discussion that took place, the theological reflection on a Calvin and Hobbes comic strip encouraged these high school students to be active in environmental issues and to take heart in being a part of a bigger landscape of activists and the earth itself yearning for healing and nourishment.

Interreligious Contexts

Although theological reflection through the lens of parables originated in the Christian understanding of parables, it does not limit the ability for dialogue across religious traditions. I have been encouraged by both Jewish and Muslim students who affirm that this lens is wide enough for interreligious reflection. Foley in his book *Reflective Believing* discusses the importance of approaching an interreligious reflection with "holy envy" and longing to learn from the other with a sense of admiration and respect. "Holy envy is humility in an appreciative mode" (2015, 75). When participants are encouraged to consider what is familiar and how their story ties into the story of their faith, the lens of parables provides an entry point for participants to draw from the parables or parabolic phrases from their own sacred texts and traditions. One of my students shared that being able to draw from her own parables in the Qur'an and sharing their wisdom with the small group felt like a safe space to breathe and be known. Because she and her classmates held a space of "holy envy" for one another, it was a welcome surprise. She pointed to the parable in the Qu'ran on chapter 18, verse 45 "(18:45) (O Prophet), propound to them the parable of the present life: it is like the vegetation of the earth which flourished luxuriantly when it mingled with the water that We sent down from the sky, but after that the same vegetation turned into stubble which the winds blew about. Allah alone has the power over all things."[1] The similarities between this and the parable of the man who built storehouses for his surplus grain in Luke 12:16 allows for a common starting point for discussions tapping our own sacred texts while approaching the other with a willingness to learn. Here the common recognition that the "stuff of this world" is all a gift and yet temporary, and our task is to bind ourselves to that which matters—our faith is important for interreligious reflecting.

The lens of parables from a Christian perspective has, as we have discussed, a slant that stands with the marginalized. Jesus' ministry which exemplified this slant was rooted in his own Jewish experience. The "eyes that can see" which reveal the perspective of God's desire to stand with the stranger, orphan, or widow is first found throughout the Hebrew scriptures in a variety of verses ranging from Deuteronomy 10:17–18 to Psalms 10:17–18. "For the LORD your God is God of gods and Lord of lords, the great God, mighty and awesome, who is not partial and takes no bribe, who executes justice for the orphan and the widow, and who loves the resident alien, giving them food and clothing" Deuteronomy 10:17–18 and Psalms 10:17–18 "O LORD, you will hear the desire of the meek; you will strengthen their heart, you will incline your ear to do justice for the orphan and the oppressed, so that no one on earth will strike terror again." Justice, compassion, and mercy are shared values across religious traditions, and engaging in theological reflection that recognizes this in the rich tradition of one another's sacred texts allows for dialogue rooted in respect and shared wisdom.

Drawing from our own sacred texts in theological reflection though the lens of parables allows participants to name what is familiar from their own tradition while also being open to learning from another's. In the effort to explore what is familiar for each member of a diverse community, each participant is exposed to the familiar lenses that another looks through, and the dialogue is fruitful. Foley's insistence on "watching our language in front of the other" (2015, 26) is a way to be cognizant of the wisdom of the other. It is often the case that the surprises in interreligious theological reflection happen when we engage the other's perspective with respect and wonder and find deep wells of wisdom from which to draw and similarities with our own traditions too.

Intercultural Contexts

Just as theological reflection in parabolic mode can be a method of interreligious dialogue, it is also a rich tool for intercultural dialogue. Jon P. Kirby, SVD, in his chapter "Building Intercultural Competence" writes, "Intercultural competence . . . is about the ongoing construction of one's reality as increasingly able to accommodate cultural difference" (*Intercultural Living*, 2015, 117). Theological reflection of any kind that engages dialogue between people from different cultures is an important tool for building intercultural competence. Theological reflection through the lens of parable offers a reminder to pay attention to what we see as familiar, and to note how that familiar points to our own cultural or contextual lenses. In recognizing our own lens, we can then engage and "accommodate" the differences we recognize in others. Critical to this type of engagement is the task of creating a sacred space for participants from diverse settings to feel confident in sharing their "familiar." Just as important is creating a sacred space for participants to gain the self-awareness needed to recognize and unpack their own contextual lenses. Often, students from a dominant culture have to be reminded that their "familiar" is tied to their own cultural or contextual lens and is not the same experience for everyone. Helping participants from dominant contexts recognize their lenses as different from another person's is the first step in encouraging intercultural competence.

In one theological reflection seminar, students were discussing a story shared by a student who visits the elderly as part of his ministry. One elder lived alone in a small apartment in a large nondescript public housing building, and he was concerned that she was lonely. As the students began sharing what was familiar to them, various students from the United States shared that their grandparents lived in nursing homes or alone in senior housing, and that they recognized the loneliness that plagued all elderly. A student from Pakistan stopped the group and said, "That loneliness, that is only familiar to you here in the US. In my home, our elders live with us and are treated as wise sages. We don't put them away in nursing homes or senior housing." The discussion continued with students from Vietnam and Mexico also sharing how elders were accommodated in their home countries. Each of them learned new perspectives from the sharing across cultures, and it also turned a lens of critique on the assumption that loneliness plagued all elderly.

Theological reflection discussions reach rich depths if participants feel that their context will be valued and respected. We talk about making sure that the voices that need to be heard are included at the table. Foley talks about silence as one of the most important ways to approach reflection with people from different contexts (2015, 34–35). Theological reflection that includes voices representing, among other things, a diversity of cultures or religious traditions or ages or genders provides a rich and surprising dialogue if all are able to participate fully. In fact, if there are no diverse voices at the table, then we must consider how to raise those voices up before our theological reflection will accomplish the "unmasking" task that makes us uncomfortable, shocked, and surprised into a new way to respond to the cries of our world. If our presupposition is that theological reflection through the lens of parables offers the space to be "parabled" by a new vision, then the work of the Spirit happens best when different perspectives are valued and sought out as reflective partners.

Nonreligious Contexts

The lens of parables can play a role in reflective discussions in a multitude of nonreligious settings as well. Small groups that have gathered around a shared value—such as a neighborhood food pantry or a beachfront cleanup—can have reflective conversations with one another about how to plan and envision their collaboration. The first step is to begin by naming the group's shared goals and values, which in turn becomes the foundation on which to build their collaborative effort. If the goal is to develop a community garden that provides the local food pantry with fresh produce, the shared values might include the desire to provide quality fresh produce, or community building which engages neighbors in gardening with one another or beautifying the abandoned lot at the corner of the neighborhood. Each of these values lined up with the main goal provide the starting point for participants. In planning projects such as this, we can too quickly move to the logistics: who can donate what, who is willing to do this or that. But we have neglected to see the role reflective dialogue plays in building the shared space of community: developing trust between participants, and fostering a sense of shared mission regardless of the language of faith. By pausing the group at various points in their time together to simply ask, what is familiar here, what is surprising, and how does that invite us to do things differently, we not only accomplish the goals at hand, but our time together becomes sacred sharing and abundantly nourishing.

This lens for reflecting can also be used in corporate settings as well. I was reading an article "Expanding the Conversation: Twenty-two Engineering Firms Lead an Effort to Promote Industry Wide Progress on Diversity and Inclusion" in the Spring 2020 issue of *Engineering Inc.*, an industry publication of the American Council of Engineering Companies (ACEC). Although Engineering publications are not my normal reading material, I had picked it up because my brother, Doug McKeown, was one of the CEOs featured in the article. As I read, I was struck by the patterns of reflective practice that were evident in their work. So, I invited my brother to have a conversation about the process on the hunch that the parabolic lens was intuitively a part of their reflective work and perhaps could offer an additional lens for their continued collaboration. The industry-wide effort had one strand of its germination in a presentation he made at the annual conference in 2018. He had agreed to share some thoughts on his own work as CEO of Woodard & Curran around the topic of diversity and inclusion at an ACEC gathering. He had agreed to do this, not because he felt he was already doing incredible work in this area, but because it offered him a chance to dig a little deeper into and learn about this issue as well as learn what practices others in the industry were trying. He asked a couple of colleagues who were women to join him in the presentation, and out of that others approached them with the thought of presenting the same topic to the Design Professional Coalition, a group of sixty of the larger engineering firms. The outcome was the formation of a working group on this issue. In all, there were twenty-three participants representing twenty-two firms who came together to form a Diversity and Inclusion Working Group (DIWG). They divided the group into three subgroups of seven or eight participants and set about trying to survey where companies thought they were in the process, gain an understanding of the current outcomes of these efforts, and to share best practices. The DIWG surveyed ACEC members, engaged in one-to-one mentoring and idea sharing, and produced a report, "Diversity and Inclusion: Keys to Success and Lessons Learned." Their work is ongoing; however, the article covered its inception, the work that took place over the course of a couple of years, meeting both remotely and in one face-to-face gathering, and the resulting report.

I started out by asking McKeown what he saw as the underlying value of their efforts. When you take the language of God out of reflective practice, the ability to focus on an ultimate value provides focus and direction. So, we began by exploring their ultimate value. I was interested in the working group's focus on diversity and inclusion and wondered if the ultimate value of being in a "right relationship" (a way of describing justice) was at the core of their work. McKeown agreed, noting that relationships had power, and the way you formed relationships in workplace culture impacted everything. Even simple conversations around sports had an ability to exclude or include others and affected the culture of inclusion. The language of justice might not have been on the lips of any of the working group as they collaborated, but creating a culture of diversity and inclusion revolves around building strong relationships that are oriented toward one another in justice. As he averred, "Relationships still come back to trust; if the tone at the top is one of trust and vulnerability, then we can together explore how to progress toward doing the right thing."

I was also struck by their use of the practice in reflective settings to divide large groups down to smaller discussion groups. Small groups become fertile ground for honesty, trust, and sharing vulnerabilities. McKeown noted, "Diversity and inclusion is a delicate topic. When it is first brought up, there can be a tendency for someone to feel defensive, as if we are questioning their moral fiber. But if we can begin with our own failures and mistakes [and] name how we have learned from them, then we can set the tone for trust and collaboration." As we have discussed earlier in this book, the starting by recognizing our own vulnerabilities is an important piece of reflective practice, and it fosters an openness to critiquing our own lenses if others model it first. McKeown named a pattern he saw in the members as they embarked on this conversation at the industry-wide level, "I would say there is a pattern or stages that each of us goes through. It starts with a feeling of defensiveness, but then as others share what has or has not worked from their own efforts, then there is a move to openness. Through that we can begin to learn and understand the depths of change we are striving for, that lead to insights, and then an ah-ha moment. It is there that we move beyond change to transformation." I resonated with his use of the word transformation. He noted that change is one step, but it becomes transformation when it is integrated into our heads and hearts. This is the move toward a heart of hospitality, which we explored in earlier chapters, and is evident in his language and the group's commitment.

When I asked him what was familiar ground or what went as expected in all of this, he started out by naming that pattern. With each conversation among the peers in the working group or with others in the industry, he recognized his own journey through these stages, and was willing to accompany others through theirs. He also noted the familiar reality that the tone at the top and a corporate culture that values diversity and inclusion impacts the whole corporation. Beyond just looking at hiring practices, they knew their work had to include a hard look at promotions, bonuses, working teams, and even casual conversations and gatherings. They also recognized that they could not simply work toward policy changes. He noted, "policies can change, priorities can change, but values don't." Their efforts had to challenge the embedded value systems to place significance on the value of relationships of inclusion. He pointed to the reality that this type of corporate value system is not only the right thing to do, but over time it also influences the effectiveness of the corporations and their productivity too. Another thing he noticed that was familiar was the easy willingness to share among the various corporations in the industry. "Even if a firm had tried only one thing, but that was extremely creative, they shared it, and we all learned from each other." The commitment to enter into the conversations with one another and to try to produce something that would impact the industry was something that he had seen in other aspects of their work and was glad to see it spill over into the tough work of diversity and inclusion.

Next I asked him to consider what surprised or challenged him throughout this process. He noted that in some cases, the firms that were supposedly further along on this stuff had not actually moved beyond policy change. "There is a difference between personal passion and how you wire it into the fiber of the organization," he noted. "We have to bring everyone along with us in order for it to become a corporate value." He also noted that the pattern toward transformation is not something that can be short circuited.

"You can't skip any of the steps. Bringing people along means recognizing and wrestling with the defensiveness and vulnerability which moves to openness and insights."

He also named a couple of surprises for him personally. Although diversity and inclusion had become a passion of his during his tenure at Woodard & Curran, he realized in looking at the firm's mission statement, which remains unchanged since it was written in 1979, that it was rooted in the same core values. "What struck me was that the language of inclusion (at least in terms of the language use of 1979) was embedded in the firm's statements and priorities, and we were building on a culture that valued this already." The terms D&I just were not what was used in 1979. It was empowering and, in some senses, humbling for him to realize that he was standing on the shoulders of others who held these same values and that they already were integral to the corporate culture he continued to cultivate.

Another surprise he realized was that he could have communicated some of the efforts he had been doing in his own firm sooner. He noted that he had perhaps held back for a couple of reasons—trying to be modest and not overwhelm others with ideas before they had had a chance to explore their own best practices, but also perhaps from a stance of being apprehensive or self-conscious; as his own data was coming in, he shouldn't have been afraid of the results. An example of this is that he—for four years running at this point—had his HR team conduct a gender and ethnic bias analysis on all pay raises, bonuses, and promotions. He had been looking to see if there were correlations between the efforts that he was trying to promote throughout the corporation and the actual practices that were being implemented, or worse, biases that were working against the D&I efforts. His sense was that if he shared that too widely with his employees, it could be seen as self-serving for the D&I efforts versus a true desire to gauge how the firm was doing in this regard. But he later recognized that it might have been more productive to share this best practice with employees because it was an example to be proud of and a statement on the types of commitments they had for changing biases within the firm.

The final piece of the lens of parables for reflective practice is to seek out the ways that the surprising moments are invitations to move further toward the Good News. In this case, how were the surprises breakthrough insights that moved the DIWG and McKeown himself to further commitment or development of their focus to build right relationships around diversity and inclusion? Immediately he noted the constantly evolving nature of the whole process. "We revised constantly to try to really capture the value of what we were learning." Working groups, such as the one here, benefit from the same discipline of the pastoral spiral. Every action breeds opportunities to reflect and learn, which in turn leads to new actions for continual revision. He noted the value of such evolution grounded in a stance of vulnerability. "If more people are willing to jump in and start without having to be perfect, then everyone is comfortable contributing and learning." Such constantly evolving practices included the need to think and rethink how to move beyond a single passionate person in a company to shifting corporate culture and industry practices. "It's not enough to assume that if leadership values this, then the whole corporation will. We had to look at how next level management is following through, how we put our money toward this—moving from asking volunteers to sit on committees, to dedicating full time employees with this as their job description."

The other surprising moment for McKeown was his own insights into the culture of inclusion already written into the founding of Woodard & Curran. He noted the invitation as that although "we've done a lot of good things already, the challenge for me is to take it to the next level." He also pointed out that this is not something that you can check off on a list of things to do; there is a commitment on his part to resourcing and nurturing this work going forward. The humility that looks at where we could be rather than only focusing all the great places we have been is refreshing and open to the parabolic critique. It also brought him back to the pattern he noted and the surprising reality that you can't skip any of the steps. Each new insight is hewn in the pattern of humility, openness, new learning, and new perspectives. Sharing those insights, being open to the lessons learned, and continuing to push a corporation and an industry forward are at the very heart of the work of the DIWG.

A group of engineering corporate representatives set out to produce a set of resources and practices that could be shared to help other firms step into the waters of diversity and inclusion. They want to broadcast that the engineering community has developed a proven approach so that the industry will be seen as an inclusive industry to attract diverse talent and to encourage growth. What they also found along the way were relationships built on shared goals, trust, and respect that could cultivate the ground around the delicate issues of diversity and inclusion with an eye on justice too. The surprising presence of reflective practices within the engineering industry is an invitation for me and any of us to consider how reflection through the lens of parables can be creatively adapted to produce Good News and shared values of hope and justice in any industry.

In the Context of Crisis

This type of foundational work that encourages groups to create a shared space of trust and mutuality is critical when groups plan to work together over a year or more. Every group goes through a series of stages as it develops and collaborates over time. Bruce Tuckman in his Forming, Storming, Norming, Performing, and Adjourning theory, which he began to develop in 1965, noted that every group goes through these stages. A group's foundational work, that includes goal setting and values sharing, makes up the beginning stage of forming. Inevitably, every group will go through what he calls the "storming" stage, when the honeymoon has worn off and people's imperfections come into high relief. Disagreements and differences of style result in chaos. By carving out the space for shared reflection and relationship building at the beginning of a collaborative effort, groups have laid a strong foundation that they can draw from as they navigate these storms. The storms themselves may be explored as surprising narratives that offer new perspectives and ways to work together toward shared goals.

In addition to helping with organizational storms, theological reflection through the lens of parables also offers a profound opportunity to reflect on how we see God in the midst of the storms of life. Suffering or crisis are moments that create profound dissonance, and choosing to reflect in a group of friends, family, or colleagues can provide glimpses of Grace that open a path forward in hope. One caveat with this type of sharing is that we can tend to turn the reflective discussion into a self-help group where we try to solve the problems brought up. Theological reflection is not meant to be a group therapy session. Groups appreciate it when they find a balance between sharing their vulnerabilities in moments of crisis and staying focused on the goal of meaning making.

In one theological reflection group, a colleague shared that his father was slipping down the road of dementia, and he was struggling to make sense of this terrible disease. He shared a story of trying to find new ways to relate to his father and being caught off guard when his father started to recite the rosary. The two of them had never prayed the rosary together. As far as he could remember, he had never seen his father with a rosary in his hands—his mother would pray the rosary when she was alive, but never his father. But his father seemed to remember all of the words, and he felt a renewed comfort reciting the rosary together.

As the group reflected together on his story, they started with the familiarity in the contextual sources. They shared a number of familiar points about dementia and its devastating effects both physically and emotionally on patients and their families. They also looked into why some patterns such as prayers or songs are easier to remember over time. They discussed relationships between fathers and sons and the reversal of roles now that he was the caretaker for his father. As they moved to what was familiar in scripture and tradition, they discussed the rosary and the mantra of the repetition of the prayers as comforting. They talked about the various saints who spent time with lepers and other outcasts. The scripture stories that came to mind were plentiful, including the commandment to honor one's father and mother and the parable of the prodigal son.

The storyteller asked the group to spend a little more time with the story of the prodigal son. As the group explored the familiar pieces of that particular parable, they observed the son asking for his inheritance early, as if his father was already gone, or perhaps wishing he were already gone. This surprising comparison brought the storyteller the realization that by focusing on his feelings of loss he was missing precious time with his father. He felt an invitation to recognize that the ability to sit and pray together was precious time. In reflecting on this, not only did he realize a connection once again to his father, but also to his mother. The group played a little with the image of the mother in the parable, perhaps standing in the house encouraging the father to run to greet his son, and that opened up a glimpse of Grace in the heart of the participant. With a renewed sense of his mother's presence encouraging the actions of his father, he felt that praying the rosary could be a way to be family despite all of the loss. Because he opened himself up to the insights and perspectives of the group, played a little with the scriptures, and allowed himself to be surprised by the movement of the Spirit, he found his heart strengthened for the road ahead. He caught glimpses of Grace in the midst of the reflection, but more importantly, in his time with his father. A willingness to share vulnerabilities even in moments of crisis and chaos, perhaps especially in moments of crisis or chaos, is essential to theological reflection through the lens of parables.

Reflection in Tune to Those at the Margins

I would like to offer one final example of how theological reflection through the lens of parables catches glimpses of God at work. This one also brings up the reminder theological reflection offers those in power to value and seek out the contributions of those on the margins. The context of the story comes from my home parish in the Archdiocese of Chicago. We were participating in the *Christ Renews His Parish* program that the Archdiocese facilitated for each parish. As pastoral associate at the time, I, along with the pastor, generated a list of potential people to serve on the team. We were required to have thirty volunteers, willing to meet weekly for thirteen weeks, to discuss the vision of our parish. We tried to make sure that we had representatives from different parts of our parish community—elderly, school families, youth, representatives of the different cultures in the parish, and so on. Although the Archdiocese did not name the ongoing gatherings as theological reflection, I was intent on making sure the space created was sacred and welcoming for fruitful reflection. Thus, for our first gathering we invited everyone to a dinner to set the tone of community building, hospitality, and lives of compassion.

One of the first people to arrive the night of our first gathering was a young man named Bill. However, Bill was not someone on our carefully cultivated list of volunteers. He had somehow heard there was food at this meeting, and whenever there was food, Bill made sure to be there. You see, Bill lived in a group home for men with developmental disabilities, and he loved to eat! Whenever there was a party at the parish, his case worker would call me up and say Bill was coming in with money for his ticket. Whenever we had coffee and donuts after masses on a weekend, Bill would ask for a half dozen or so to "bring back to the guys." Seeing Bill at an event that included food was about as predictable as the sunrise. So, I should not have been surprised by his arrival in the church hall that night, but I was. We had not advertised this on the parish calendar, but somehow he knew there was food.

When he got his food and settled down at a table, I had to laugh. Clearly, we had missed including some voices that were supposed to be at the table. Bill wasn't the only person in the community with learning disabilities; in fact, there were several group homes in the area and a large residential program for women with Down's Syndrome. People from each of those places were regular members of our community. We also had a SPRED program, which is a special religious education program for persons with learning disabilities. Bill's presence was a clear reminder that our visioning and planning over the next thirteen weeks had to include their perspective as well.

At one point, as more and more people arrived for the meeting, the pastor pulled me aside and asked, "What do we do about Bill?" I smiled and said, "We make sure to have food at every meeting," and then shared with him my thoughts about how important his presence would be for our parish visioning. Bill came to every meeting, I always made enough cookies or zucchini bread so he could "bring some home to the guys," and as per his regular patterns, he never said a word in the group discussions. But his presence spoke volumes and reminded all of us to celebrate and continue to envision our community as a place of hospitality and compassion.

The Spirit moves in surprising ways to remind us to listen with ears that can hear and see with eyes that can see. When we are open to the surprises, willing to be shifted out of our comfort zones, and compassionate enough to be led to solidarity, then we have been parabled!

NOTE

1. This translation of the Qur'an is from Islamicstudies.info. (http://www.islamicstudies.info/tafheem.php/?sura=18&verse=45) Last accessed on May 27, 2020.

Epilogue
Finding Hope in Family during COVID-19

As I was writing this book, our world became engulfed in the COVID-19 pandemic. The "shelter at home" recommendations that went into effect in the United States in mid-March 2020 shifted all manner of life as schools transitioned to digital learning, businesses shut down, and people focused on "flattening the curve" and the dwindling supply of personal protective equipment.

The Bernardin Center at Catholic Theological Union decided to accompany our larger community through a weekly discussion series titled "A People of Hope." Steve Millies, the director of the Bernardin Center, asked various faculty members to host these evenings and he reached out to me to ask if I could focus on *Finding Hope in Family during COVID-19*. Below is the transcript of that evening. I saw it as a theological reflection through the lens of parables on our moment in time and I share it here as a closing statement on Parabolic Hope:

Welcome! Welcome to those of you present this evening and those watching in the future. When Steve first asked me if I would speak tonight, my first thoughts were "please no—I have no time! And no real answers on how to find hope right now, I'm trying to navigate all of this too." But my sister suggested that perhaps no one is looking for answers, but just to know we are not alone in our questions. And what we all needed most was just a reminder to look for the silver lining of this moment, to look for where we see the Spirit is at work. And then I realized it was the week of Mother's Day and felt Nudged by the Spirit to do this in honor of Mother's Day for my own mother—whom I know is here with us tonight, and for all those—no matter their gender—who mother others with their love and companionship. So Happy Mother's Day everyone!

Let us begin. Who am I and what do I have to offer tonight? Here at CTU I am the director of Field Education and I also teach courses on pastoral ministry and spirituality, and particularly family spirituality. But before that, I am a wife and mother. My husband Chris and I have four children who are now twenty-four, twenty-two, eighteen, and sixteen. And they are the love of our lives. And before all of that, I am a child of James and Evelyn McKeown and part of a large extended family. My parents are in their 80s and I am the sixth of eight children. So, I promise to share stories from all of these experiences of family—that will hopefully highlight glimpses of the Spirit at work even in these strange times.

Our task at hand—Finding hope in Family during COVID-19. Wow, that is an interesting task that each of us must take up. Family life is messy and complex and even in a fairly healthy family, the layers of anxiety and stress that have been added since the beginning of March make all of the warts and imperfections come into high relief. Finding a balance with all of the variables at play has become nearly impossible. I think of the parents who have little ones trying to balance working at home with the sudden role of teacher and constant playmate for their little ones. I am mindful of friends and colleagues whose adult children are not at home and their worries are constant. And my niece and nephew who are expecting their first child next week or others who are attending to the needs of elderly parents with health issues that have become more complicated during this time. Our prayers go out to the families who are impacted by this pandemic either as a health issue or an economic issue or both. This is tough stuff. Whether you are in a family or minister to families, your task in this moment has gotten exponentially harder for a variety of reasons.

If you work with families and you find you're curious, I would recommend that you pick one issue families deal with and trace it through this pandemic. Pick one issue—addiction, anxiety, immigration, domestic violence, child abuse, the way this pandemic disproportionately impacts people of color—and pay attention; see what is being said about it in the news or in the social media. Notice what is not being said about it. Try to build up your skill set for how you minister to families experiencing this issue.

An issue I volunteer with in my parish is Domestic Violence. The amount of calls to Domestic Violence emergency help lines has increased so much during this pandemic. I've asked Peter to put up the number and chat link online for the National Domestic Violence Hotline (1-800-799-7233 or www.thehotline.org). Please make sure to post this number and link in forums you are able to—in your newsletter or on your parish website or social media. Check for the local hotline numbers for your area and post those. Or if you are listening tonight and this is an experience in your own home, please know there are people ready to help. Pope Francis says in *Amores Laetitia*, "The triune God is a communion of Love, and the family is its living reflection." Domestic Violence has no place in a family; violence is not a reflection of

God's love. Yet we unfortunately deal with it in overwhelming amounts around the world, across all cross-sections of culture and economic status. When I think about sheltering at home I feel tremendous grief for those for whom home is not a safe place, and our parish domestic violence committee struggles to figure out how we continue to stay present and prayerful around this issue now.

That is what makes this moment particularly hard—we each have to face the question: "What do I have to offer?" These issues are huge and we are sheltering at home; what do we do for others that really matters right now?

And in the midst of wrestling with those larger feelings of limitations, I find myself also navigating the complexities of family life in my own family in the chaos of COVID-19. Let me give you a quick snapshot of our household.

My husband and I are both teachers, me here at CTU and he at a Catholic High School. Like so many others, we both had to quickly move all of our work into the digital realm. My oldest son is also a teacher—a middle school science teacher for a Chicago Public School and as the shelter at home orders went into effect, he decided to move back home rather than shelter on his own. I also have two students who are in college—one who won't be having a graduation ceremony until all of this is behind us and both of them were quickly returned home as schools closed. My daughter had been studying abroad in Ghana, so her return home on March 17 was full of anxiety. My youngest has moved her high school junior year with its major focus on college preparations to the digital realm as well, so at any given moment in our house we have three teachers teaching and three students working and it is more than just the bandwidth on our internet that is stretched to capacity. Each of them is stretching their proverbial wings and yet here we are together in spaces of childhood patterns over long stretches of time that layer on interesting new ways to build relationships.

Don't get me wrong, I know our family life is much easier than it is for others, but even before all of the chaos hit, I had already been wrestling with the usual concerns parents of young adults have—are they living lives of virtue, how are they discerning major life choices, or is their spiritual life thriving? And in this moment, there is a juxtaposition of more time to spend together, but without the familiar patterns of life. The segway into conversations of faith is hard. We have to intentionally think through being a domestic church—and to think it through with young adults is a different picture than thinking it through with toddlers or teens. As parents, we have to pay attention to what symbols hold meaning for our children and how do they implicitly or explicitly showcase our shared values. Also, when we look at family spirituality we have to figure out the ways each person thrives and grows independently but also interdependently within the whole. Thus, a need to figure out new ways of making the faith we value tangible and meaningful to our children. I don't know if I have any answers to any of those questions, but I have learned with the help of friends and family to listen rather than ask, to trust in the Spirit rather than worry.

In this space of patient listening, I have become profoundly hopeful. Reminded that we are a people of hope [that] we have a responsibility to be. Pope Francis also says, "The most important task of families is to provide an education in hope." Families provide an education in hope not only for our children, but for the communities around us too. We teach each generation what hope looks like, feels like, and tastes like. The hope itself comes from God, but like new buds in springtime, we cultivate the spaces and the possibilities to catch a glimpse of hope. Hopefully some of the stories I tell tonight will help you catch a glimpse of the hope that lives within you and your family.

I love theological reflection rooted in parables and I am always looking for the moments of surprise that flip us on our heads in everyday life. I see surprises as God's way of getting our attention, breaking in and catching us off guard with a new way to see. The oft-repeated phrase of "having eyes that can see," we might even call it "having sacramental eyes," is the challenge to see things the way God might see them. I look for moments of surprise as ways to notice God breaking through and inviting us to embody hope, to collaborate in God's Good News.

So, let me start with one story from when my children were little: I was so in love with them and I wanted to never forget that they were a complete gift from God so I used to scoop them up at any moment and ask "Who said you could be so cute?" And I had taught them to respond "God." It was my own little prayer and reminder to thank God for their joy. So, I would scoop them up and kiss them on their heads and ask, "Who said you could be so cute?" and they would squirm away saying, "God!" One day, my son Josh, who was about two years old at the time, was out in the back yard running around in the rain in nothing but his socks. I was mortified! So, I went out onto the back deck and yelled, "Josh, get up here!" And as he got close, I scolded him saying, "Who said you could go outside?" He looked up and said, "God!" He had no idea what he was saying at that moment, he was just parroting what I had taught him to say to any "who said" question. But for me it was a surprising invitation to enjoy that spring rain with the heart of a delightful child.

That is a story I tell often. If you have had me in class or came to one of my talks you have probably heard that one. But as I was planning for tonight thinking about surprising moments in the last couple of months, I realized that I cannot shape the narrative anymore. I can't teach them what to say, or how to act, and yet, I can still listen for how God breaks through to shape and reshape me into an authentic example of God's love with the heart of a delightful child.

So, I have learned to not force the narrative; I've learned again in these last few weeks to listen and trust and hold a stance of wonder and awe, ever ready to be surprised by glimpses of God in the most ordinary of moments.

On first glance, this pandemic has all of us in one way or another looking at life as if there is a limit to the good news available. Whether it is a limit on the toilet paper at the store, or a limit to our time, or a limit to our capacity to navigate this moment. But I am trying to go from a position of limited good where I feel drained and have nothing to offer to being, as Pope Francis says in *Evangelii Gaudiuma,* "fearlessly open to the work of the Spirit."

I would like to pause us here for a moment and ask a question. Just reflect and maybe jot it down for yourself. I am going to ask several questions as we go along, and then in the end, perhaps we can continue the discussion by having you answer some of these questions as a way to share with one another our moments of Hope. So, our first question is:

What do you linger on? What images or sounds catch your attention and cause you to pause? Why? My colleague Eileen Crowley says photography is a spiritual practice. What is it you have found yourself taking pictures of these last few weeks?

We can choose to linger on images of hope or images of diminished good. Our faith invites us to linger on those images of hope to nurture our spirituality. As I reflected on the surprising glimpses of hope, I started to notice patterns that were worth naming and celebrating. And they felt to me not only like sacramental moments, but truly like sacraments and gifts of the Holy Spirit.

First, I would like to name Community. I know we all have been amazed at the ability to connect with loved ones or friends across place and time. My classes were quickly shifted to Zoom sessions, and at one point a student led the class in prayer using a common phrase. He said, "Dear God, thank you for joining us in this place" and I thought how true! Of course, God has joined us in our digital spaces too. No matter where we are right now, we are together in the spirit; the same is true for us tonight, we claim that as a people of faith we are connected with those across spaces and those who have gone before us across time.

A simpler example of community across time was the beautiful surprise of my daughter Josie's digital choir concert; all of the students recorded their own piece of the harmony on their own and their choir teacher blended them all together into the complete song. It was amazing to hear them sing together from different spaces and recorded at different times yet harmonizing beautifully in a spirit-filled moment. That is community across space and time, but we also work on building community right in our own homes. The busyness of family back in one house doesn't take away from the need to be intentional about building community again with our spouse or with our family. It is the simple reconnecting that happens in our own spaces too that are extraordinary. When my daughter arrived back home from Ghana, each of my other children found their own times and spaces to reconnect with her; a twosome here in the hammock, or another two curled up on the couch in the basement or cooking together in the kitchen. Each of them built their relationships up again with this newfound time and renewed their sense of being a community.

So, I ask: How are you surprised by community forming in this moment? What relationships have you renewed across time and space?

And about that cooking together in the kitchen. Everything about food is a sacred connection to the Eucharistic celebration. My neighbor and then my sister and then a colleague each pointed out how they are lingering longer at the dinner table. I was surprised that they each used the exact words. "We are lingering longer at dinner." And it's true in my house too. During the day we are all pretty consumed with schoolwork, but by dinner time, we have congregated in the kitchen to prepare a meal and sit around the table to eat and chat and laugh. We linger there longer, sharing stories and cracking jokes. Eventually the Star Wars trivia gives way to hopes and dreams and I am reminded again and again that the Eucharist happens when we nourish one another with our lives.

So, I ask: What are ways meals have become Eucharistic celebrations for you in these moments? How are they moments that nourish your soul? And how can our day of fasting and prayer on May 14 be a continuation of our Eucharistic communion with those hurting around the world?

There are traces of the sacraments of vocation and discernment if we pay attention, too. My daughter who has just graduated is still wrestling with finding a job in this moment and discerning who she wants to be. And my oldest is a second-year teacher still settling into his own sense of calling. One of my favorite things to do each day is to eavesdrop on him as he teaches his sixth, seventh, and eight grade students. He is amazingly dedicated, and I love to hear him with his students. I am amazed at how perfectly he has found his vocation. And also how he works to help his students lean into who they could be, too. Each morning he starts out with his "bell ringer" (the simple conversation that they start with at the beginning of each day) and his bell ringer a couple of days ago was for each of his students to type in the chat box their answers to his questions: "What is your superhero name and what is your superpower?" He wasn't asking "if they were superheroes, what would their names be," he was just assuming they already knew they were one!" A fun exercise no doubt, but also an empowering one. Who we become is opened up before us when others expect us to have superpowers, or at least to dream!

What are you dreaming about these days? What would you answer if our teacher asked us: "What is your superhero name, and what is your superpower?"

We see moments of reconciliation too. As hard as we try to be patient in arguments, we still have moments where we need to say I'm sorry, and showing up with a cool glass of lemonade, or baking—seems to help. Sweets are good conduits for smoothing down frustrations in our house. My daughter, Evie, loves to bake and the smells waft through the house pulling us all close for a taste. Baking is also a good metaphor for how reconciliation and compassion are bound together. We have to be vulnerable, broken down, kneaded together, shaped, and baked into something that can nourish another.

In the moments when we share our vulnerabilities, we are able to understand compassion. The nurses and doctors and other frontline workers are all stepping into their work and they are extremely vulnerable these days. But they have always been vulnerable. I have neighbors, and nieces, and nephews who are nurses and they are always opening their hearts up to the stories of pain and grief in the lives of the people they serve. They are images of hope again and again for us because they show up, even when they are vulnerable, and show us what compassion and solidarity really mean.

How have you been surprised by the compassion of another these past few months? What has moved you or stirred you to respond with compassion?

Another gift of the Holy Spirit that I have noticed is Reverence, or what I like to call the Liturgy of the Hours of Wonder and Awe. I have never had the time to really trace the day through the patterns of nature before, but nature prays the liturgy of the hours in amazing ways! 4:30 am—it never fails; the choir of birds sing their praises of glory. Then the sun rises, slicing across the horizon with a shimmer of color; it was around 6:15 this morning. There were many days this past winter my husband and I would head out to drive different directions just as the sun was rising and we might watch it in the car on our commute—but now during these days we can watch it together. As the sun slowly moves across the sky, I love the little buds that uncurl and face it throughout the day—promising the hope of spring, and the way the sun feels on our face. I remind my children and my students, "If the sun is shining, get outside and let it kiss your cheeks! Even for 5 minutes, it will change your perspective on everything." I am intrigued by the way the breeze pauses around 6:00 pm and all the earth gets quiet with anticipation. And there have been some beautiful sunsets! All of this hope and promise mixed in with the news reports of reduced greenhouse gases and cleaner air quality have us wondering what changes in all of this can we hold onto for our mother earth!

And I ask: "What are we willing to give up and never go back to in order to join this Liturgy of the Hours of Wonder and Awe?"

Another story which I see as a liturgical sending forth is almost like an anointing. Since the start of the stay-at-home orders, my sister invited all of us to "go to mass" via livestream with her. So, my parents and siblings have now gathered in the digital space most Sunday mornings together to be the

Church. I haven't been with all of my siblings and parents at church since my parents' fiftieth anniversary mass. We are spread across the East Coast and Midwest, but this has been a lovely pattern of being together for mass. We usually have a group text going during the liturgy and we text our shared petitions and our "Peace be with you's" to each other. We might even comment on the outstanding music or an insight from the homily. One of the first times that we gathered for mass, at the end of the liturgy, the priest, probably still a little awkward with recording this in his empty church, forgot to say the sending rite. I almost didn't notice that it was missing. But then my Mom texted, "Go now in peace to love and serve the Lord!" And it brought me to tears. How fitting it was that she was sending us from our domestic church; a mother sending her children to love and serve.

And I find myself asking all of us: can we name ways we have been sent during this pandemic? Or what are the ways you send others to love and serve the Lord during this time?

So, I have learned that I can no longer try to shape the narrative of my family with parroted answers to a "who said" question, but I can trust the Spirit is at work in them and in each of us and I can work to be a part of that sending forth in hope and expectation.

I have one last story from our sacred texts (kind of!) As I was thinking through this reflection and letting scripture passages come to mind. The miracle of Jesus feeding the 5,000 (not counting women and children as the scripture claims) stood out. It's a story where the disciples were seeing things from the perspective of limited goods ("we only have three loaves and a few fish"). And the miracle was something that challenged them to see the possibilities of abundant hope.

I love that story, except tonight I want to tell it this way. It is the *miracle of Jesus making a million masks.* You see my neighbor asked if I had any cotton fabric lying around because she and her ten-year-old daughter wanted to make masks for people. The fabric stores were closed, but they wanted to get started on them. So, I went to my closet and pulled out a bunch of remnants from projects through the years and dropped off a shopping bag full of scraps. My sister in Ohio was doing the same thing, and she sent a link for a site matching seamstresses with those who needed masks, so we compared patterns and set to work. We modified patterns to find a good fit and modified again as we ran out of elastic. As the first ones were done, my neighbor would facetime or send a picture. Her daughter was excited to show her work. And each time I saw a finished mask or worked on one myself I would think, "Oh, that was Evie's clown costume from Halloween in third grade," or "That was the remnant of Josh's shepherd outfit when he was in the school Christmas pageant," or "That was from the Easter dresses the girls wore years ago." And I realized that there were women and children (yes, we are counting the women and children in this one!) truly, people all over the world doing this same thing. What else could we do that would matter? We worked, and sheltered at home, and tried to make a mask or two when we had the time. But the reality is that Jesus is making a million masks. You see God takes these bits and scraps of who we are and binds us with one another and shapes us into gifts for those in need. And each of us, through the mantra of sewing, or listening, teaching our kids, or caring for an elderly parent, are sharing the bits and scraps of who we are and together becoming a people of Hope, a light in the darkness, a domestic church that shares the Eucharist abundantly across time and space.

If our teacher asks, "What is your superpower?" As a people of faith, today and everyday I'd say our superpower is "Hope!"

Amen!

Appendix A
Theological Reflection in Parabolic Mode

PRELIMINARY OUTLINE OF METHOD

Discussion points to frame the reflection:
- God is present throughout our lives
- Parables point to the reign of God
- Parables are always Good News for the marginalized
- Parables have aspects that are familiar, make sense, and comfortable
- Parables have aspects that are surprising, shocking, or challenging
- Parables are open ended—waiting for a response
- Theological reflection works best if we are open to the process
- Theological reflection works best in a community willing to discern together and challenge one another

Steps:

1. Naming an experience
   - Name any recent experience that comes to mind
   - Frame it as a story complete with a beginning/middle/end
   - Describe the steps taken, feelings that arose, and/or thoughts that crossed your mind
   - Note ways in which you were an observer
   - Note ways in which you were an active participant in this experience
2. Exploring the experience as a community
   - Allow each participant to see how their own experiences are similar or different
   - Together brainstorm parables or stories in the life of Jesus that are similar to the experience

- Select one parable or story to explore alongside the experience as you move through the rest of the reflection
- Lay out the ways the experience and the parable are similar or different
3. Recognizing the familiar
    - What do we observe as familiar in the experience?
    - What is comfortable?
    - What makes sense about the way people act or respond in this experience? What is "to be expected?"
    - Why do these responses make sense—are responses based on past experiences, on the way "things are done," or on the expectations people or culture have?
    - How are the familiar pieces of this experience similar to the familiar pieces of the parable chosen?
4. Seeking the surprise
    - What do we observe as surprising in this experience? What was uncomfortable?
    - What happened that was not what we expected? What challenged us because it turned our expectations upside down?
    - Why were these pieces surprising or shocking? Where have the expectations of people or culture been turned upside down?
    - Did anything happen that was shocking? If not, why not?
    - How are the shocking pieces of this experience similar to the shocking pieces of the parable chosen?
5. Acknowledging the invitation
    - As an observer—we strive to see where God moves in the experience, we strive to recognize the kingdom of God.
        - Who or what showed the movement of God in the parable you chose? How is that similar or different from the experience?
        - What about the surprises in your experience give insight into God's movement—or the reign of God?
        - What about the experience that challenges us or invites us to respond with Good News for the marginalized?
        - How might we have seen differently?
        - How do we see God inviting us into relationship?
    - As participants—we strive to understand our actions as our response to God, actions that are Good News for the marginalized—building the reign of God.
        - Where was the Good News in the parable you choose? How is that similar or different from the experience?
        - How do the things that surprised us in our experience invite us to cultivate Good News?
        - How did our actions resemble the Good News?

- How could our actions have been more surprising—more in line with the Good News?
- What might we have done differently?
- How do we see our actions as part of our relationship with God?
6. Responding to the invitation
    - What insights or challenges will you hold on to from this reflection?
    - How does this reflection impact your actions in the future?
    - How does this reflection help you to recognize God in the midst of the world?
    - How does this reflection help you name how you might respond to God with your life?
    - How do we or could we as a community celebrate the responses that are Good News?
    - Do we see ourselves as co-workers with God building the reign?
    - Name concrete ways your actions or observations will change in the future.
    - How can the frame of parables shape the way we respond to such experiences in the future?

© Christina R. Zaker, D.Min.

Appendix B
High School Service Journal

Service Project Journal

Please complete this top portion and have it signed by your site supervisor on the day of the project. You have one week from the day of the project to complete the journal below.

Student Name: Student Email:

Graduation year: Date of service:

Service Project Site: Signature of Supervisor:

Respond to at least one question in each section
You are free to use more paper to answer more questions
if you wish to.

When we engage in service work, it is helpful to think about what is familiar to us about the experience. We do this by considering what we know about the activity we are undertaking, the place where we are doing it, and the people with whom we work. We also consider our own perspectives.
Describe the service project:
- Who were the people you met and worked with during this project?
- What does this organization do? What is its mission?
- What did you do during your time there?
- Use your senses: what did you see, hear, smell, touch, or taste in your time there?

Consider your perspectives:
- What are the reasons you decided to volunteer with this particular project?
- How did you feel as you prepared for, engaged in, or headed home from this project?
- Would you do this again? Why or why not?
- As you think back on the experience now, what do you think others might have thought about your presence there?

Often when we engage in volunteering, we are surprised or caught off guard because things do not play out exactly as we expect. It is important to see that these surprises move us out of our comfort zone and help us to consider ways we can grow from this experience.

Surprises and Challenges:
- What happened that you did not expect to happen?
- What surprised you about the way people responded to you or to one another there?
- What made you uncomfortable or annoyed?
- What did you do or feel that left you embarrassed or disappointed?
- What made you laugh?
- What made you feel happy or grateful during this activity?
- If you could have grabbed your phone to take only one picture during the day, what one glimpse of the day would you capture? Why?

We engage in service activities as part of our school requirements because it offers students an opportunity to grow and learn how to respond with compassion to the needs of others.

The invitation to growth:
- As you think through your volunteer service and this journal activity, what might be the ways you have been invited to grow?
- Considering your surprise or challenge in the section above, what might you learn from the experience of moving outside of your comfort zone in this way?
- Name one person who models compassion: how did this experience help you try to be compassionate like them?

Please return the top copy of this journal to the service-learning office within one week of your volunteer service activity. All students must complete four service journals by the end of April.

Bibliography

Bevans, Stephen B. *Models of Contextual Theology*. Maryknoll, NY: Orbis Books, 1992.

Bevans, Stephen B., and Roger Schroeder. *Prophetic Dialogue: Reflections on Christian Mission Today*. Maryknoll, NY: Orbis Books, 2011.

Bloom, Matthew. "Research Insights from the Flourishing in Ministry Project," *Work Well Research*, accessed June 2, 2020, https://workwellresearch.com/media/images/FIM_Report_Flourishing_in_Ministry_2.pdf.

Buechner, Fredrich. *Wishful Thinking: A Theological ABC*. New York: Harper and Row, 1973.

Cimperman, Maria. *Social Analysis for the 21st Century*. Maryknoll, NY: Orbis Books, 2015.

Cochrane, James. *Circles of Dignity: Community Wisdom and Theological Reflection*. Minneapolis, MN: Fortress Press, 1999.

"Contemplative Dialogue," Leadership Conference of Women Religious, accessed June 2, 2020, https://lcwr.org/contemplative-dialogue.

Crossan, John Dominic. *In Parables: the Challenge of the Historical Jesus*. Sonoma, CA: Polebridge Press, 1992.

Crowder, Stephanie Buckanon. *The Dark Interval: Towards a Theology of Story*. Santa Rosa, CA: Polebridge Press, 1988.

———. *The Historical Jesus: The Life of a Mediterranean Jewish Peasant*. San Francisco, CA: Harper Collins, 1991.

———. *When Momma Speaks: the Bible and Motherhood from a Womanist Perspective*. Louisville, KY: Westminster John Knox Press, 2016.

de la Torre, Miguel A. *Handbook of U.S. Theologies of Liberation*. St. Louis, MO: Chalice Press, 2004.

de Mesa, José. *Why Theology is Never Far From Home*. Manila, Philippines: De La Salle University Press, 2003.

Dodd, C. H. *The Parables of the Kingdom*. rev. ed. London: J. Nisbet, 1961.

Donahue, John R. *The Gospel in Parable: Metaphor, Narrative, and Theology in the Synoptic Gospels.* Philadelphia, PA: Fortress, 1998.

Downey, Michael. *Understanding Christina Spirituality.* New York: Paulist Press, 1997.

Foley, Edward. *Theological Reflection Across Religious Traditions: The Turn to Reflective Believing.* Lanham, MD: Rowman & Littlefield, 2015.

Frohlich, Mary. *Breathed into Wholeness: Catholicity and Life in the Spirit.* Maryknoll, NY: Orbis Books, 2019.

Funk, Robert W. *Funk on Parables: Collected Essays.* Santa Rosa, CA: Polebridge Press, 2006.

Godzieba, Anthony J. "The Catholic Sacramental Imagination and the Access/Excess of Grace," *New Theology Review*, 2008. 14–26.

Greeley, Andrew. *The Catholic Imagination.* Los Angeles, CA: University of California Press, 2001.

Groome, Thomas. *Christian Religious Education: Sharing Our Story and Vision.* San Francisco, CA: Harper and Row, 1980.

———. *Sharing Faith: A Comprehensive Approach to Religious Education and Pastoral Ministry: The Way of Shared Praxis.* San Francisco, CA: HarperSanFrancisco, 1991.

Hennick, Calvin. "Expanding the Conversation: Twenty-two Engineering Firms Lead an Effort to Promote Industry-wide Progress on Diversity and Inclusion," Engineering Inc., Spring 2020, 2–5.

Herzog, William. *Parables as Subversive Speech: Jesus as Pedagogue of the Oppressed.* Louisville, KY: Westminster/John Knox Press, 1994.

Holland, Joe, and Peter Henriot. *Social Analysis: Linking Faith and Justice.* rev. and enl. ed. Maryknoll, NY: Dove Communications; Orbis Books in collaboration with the Center of Concern, 1983.

Imperatori-Lee, Natalia. *Cuéntame: Narrative in the Ecclesial Present.* Maryknoll, NY: Orbis Books, 2018.

John XXIII, Pope. *Mater et Magistra/ On Christianity and Social Progress.* May 15, 1961. Papal Archives. The Holy See. http://www.vatican.va/content/john-xxiii/en/encyclicals/documents/hf_j-xxiii_enc_15051961_mater.html.

John Paul II, Pope. *On Social Concern.* December 30, 1987. Papal Archives. *The Holy See*, accessed March 2, 2012, http:www.vatican.va/edocs/eng0223/_INDEX.htm.

Johnson, Elizabeth. *Consider Jesus: Waves of Renewal in Christology.* New York: Crossroad, 2010.

Johnson, Luke Timothy. *The Gospel of Luke, Sacra Pagina* 3. Collegeville, MN: The Liturgical Press, 1999.

Jones, Dewitt. "Celebrate What's Right with the World." Filmed September 2017 in South Lake Tahoe, CA. Ted Video, 18:10. https://www.ted.com/talks/dewitt_jones_celebrate_what_s_right_with_the_world?language=en.

Justes, Emma. *Hearing Beyond the Words: How to Become a Listening Pastor.* Nashville, TN: Abingdon Press, 2006.

Kinast, Robert. "Method In Ministry Review," *Theological Studies*, 1981, Vol. 42, no. 2, 343–344.

———. *What are They Saying About Theological Reflection?* New York: Paulist Press, 2000.

Kirby, SVD, Jon P. "Building Intercultural Competence," *Intercultural Living*. Vol. 1. Stanislaus and Ueffing eds. Sankt Augustin: Steyler Missionswissenschaftliches Institut; New Delhi: ISPCK, 2015.

Lamott, Anne. *Bird by Bird: Some Instructions on Writing and Life*. New York: Pantheon Books, 1994.

Lederach, John Paul. "The Moral Imagination: The Art And Soul of Building Peace Association of Conflict Resolution," *European Judeaism*, 2007, Vol. 40, no. 2, 9–21.

McBrian, Richard P. *Catholicism: New Edition*. San Francisco, CA: HarperSanFrancisco, 1994.

O'Connell Killen, Patricia, and John de Beer. *The Art of Theological Reflection*. New York: Crossroad, 1994.

———. "Assisting Adults to Think Theologically." In *Method in Ministry: Theological Reflection and Christian Ministry,* eds. James Whitehead and Evelyn Eaton Whitehead, 103–110. rev. New York: Sheed and Ward, 1995.

Ospino, Hosffman, "Theological Horizons for a Pedagogy of Accompaniment." *Religious Education*, 2010, Vol. 105, no. 4, 413–429.

Pattison, Stephen, Judith Thompson, and John Green. "Theological Reflection for the Real World: Time to Think Again." *British Journal of Theological Education*, 2003, Vol. 13, no. 2, 119–131.

Quasten, S. T. D., Johannes and Joseph C. Lumpe, PhD, eds. *Ancient Christian Writers: The Works of the Fathers in Translation*. New York: Paulist Press, 1948.

Rausch, Thomas P. *Educating for Faith and Justice: Catholic Higher Education Today*. Collegeville, MN: The Liturgical Press, 2010.

Reid, O. P., Barbara. *Parables for Preachers: Year C*. Collegeville, MN: The Liturgical Press, 2000.

Reid, Barbara, O.P., General Editor, "Wisdom Commentary," Liturgical Press, accessed June 2, 2020, https://litpress.org/wisdom-commentary-series?gclid=EAI aIQobChMIrOOG8OLj6QIVDdvACh2CuAtmEAAYASAAEgJ7_vD_BwE

Rolheiser, Ronald. *Holy Longings: The Search for a Christian Spirituality*. New York: Image, Random House, 2014.

Romero, Oscar. *The Violence of Love*. Farmington, PA: Plough Publishing House, 1998.

Schillebeeckx, Edward. *Christ: The Experience of Jesus as Lord*. Trans. John Bowden. New York: Crossroad, 1981.

———. *Church: The Human Story of God*. Trans. John Bowden. New York: Crossroad, 1993.

———. *Jesus: An Experiment in Christology*. Trans. Hubert Hoskins. New York: Seabury Press, 1979.

———. *God Among Us: The Gospel Proclaimed*. Trans. John Bowden. New York: Crossroad, 1983.

Schreiter, Robert J. *Constructing Local Theologies*. New York: Orbis Books, 2008.

Schüssler, Fiorenza. *In Memory of Her: A Feminist Theological Reconstruction of Christian Origins*, Edition 10. Spring Valley, NY: Herder & Herder, 1994.

Shalom Ministries and Community, Bevans, Stephen, Eleanor Doidge, and Robert J. Schreiter, eds. *The Healing Circle: Essays in Cross-Cultural Mission Presented to the Rev. Dr. Claude Marie Barbour*. Chicago, IL: CCGM Publications, 2000.

Snyder, Larry. *Think and Act Anew: Poverty in America Affects Us All and What We Can Do about It*. Maryknoll, NY: Orbis Books, 2010.

"Towards Understanding the Quran," *Islamic Studies*, accessed June 2, 2020, http://www.islamicstudies.info/tafheem.php/?sura=18&verse=45&to=46.

Tuckman, Bruce. "Developmental Sequence in Small Groups," *Psychological Bulletin*, 1965, Vol. 63, no. 6, 384–399.

Westley, Dick. *Good Things Happen: Experiencing Community in Small Groups*. Mystic, CT: Twenty-Third Publications, 1992.

Whitehead, James, and Evelyn Eaton Whitehead. *Method in Ministry: Theological Reflection and Christian Ministry*. rev. New York: Sheed & Ward, 1995.

Wijsen, Frans, Peter Henriot, and Rodrigo Mejía, eds. *The Pastoral Circle Revisited: A Critical Quest for Truth and Transformation*. Maryknoll, NY: Orbis Books, 2005.

Zaker, Christina. "Starting Point," *National Catholic Reporter*, 2007, Vol. 43, no. 35 edition.

Index

Amores Laetitia encyclical, 126

Barbour, Claude Marie, 37, 40
Bernardin Center at CTU, 125
Bevans, Stevan, 95–96
Bloom, Matthew, 27
Buechner, Fredrick, 91–92

Calvin and Hobbes, *112*–13
Cardijin, Cardinal Joseph, 23, 39, 45
Cimperman, Maria, 25, 42, 86n1
Cochrane, James, 82–83, 86, 96, 97
contextual lenses. *See* sources; context as source
Crossan, John Dominic, 52, 57, 59, 60, 86, 95, 97

DeBeer, John, 9–10, 24, 39, 69, 70, 91
De Mesa, José M., 25, 44–45
dialogue, 43–48; communal, 23, 68–69, 78, 95; contemplative dialogue, 96; facilitating reflective dialogue, 48; parables as, 57–59; prophetic dialogue, 96, 97, 101; as spiritual practice, 95
didache, 11–12
Dodd, CH, 50–51, 52, 59
Domestic Violence National Hotline, 126
Donahue, Fr. Scott, 66
Donahue, John R., 51–53, 59, 83

Downey, Michael, 89

Engineering Inc., 116
Evangelii Gaudium encyclical, 129

Foley, Edward, 2, 26, 27, 38, 40, 42, 93, 113–15
Frohlich, Mary, 90–91, 93–95, 97
Funk, Robert W., 60

Godzieba, Anthony J., 14, 15, 17–18
Greeley, Andrew, 65
Groome, Thomas, 30, 35, 36, 44

heart of hospitality, 26, 37–39, 77
Herzog, William, 57, 59, 85
Holland, Joe and Peter Henriot, S.J., 25, 42, 84–85, 86n1

Ignatius Loyola: Daily Examin, 32; Ignatian contemplation, 94; spiritual exercises, 94
imagination, 14–15, 17; imagining the "other" way, 18; moral, 98; poetic 17; sacramental, 11, 14, 15, 18, 27, 33, 51, 57. *See also* Godzieba, Anthony J.
Imperatori-Lee, Natalia, 10, 43

Index

intercultural contexts, 114–15. *See also* inculturation; styles of theological reflection

Johnson, Elizabeth, 60, 62, 85
Johnson, Luke Timothy, 56
Jones, Dewitt, 6, 18
Julian of Norwich, 93
Justes, Emma J., 37
Justice, 75, 85, 100, 103, 117

Kinast, Robert, 24–26, 104
Kirby, Jon P., 114

Lamott, Anne, 31–32
Laudato Sí encyclical, 112
Leadership Council of Women Religious, 95
Lederach, John Paul, 98–100
lo cotidiano, 10

McBrien, Richard, 13
McKeown, Doug, 116–20
Mercy Home for Boys and Girls, 66, 80–82

O'Connell Killen, Patricia, 9–10, 24, 39, 41, 69, 70, 91
On Social Concern encyclical, 84
Ospino, Hoffsman, 77, 83

parabled, 60–61, 73, 82, 86, 94, 115
parables, 50; as dialogue, 57–59; having "ears that can hear," 3, 15, 16, 50, 57, 60, 83, 86, 94; and justice for those on the margins 54–55, 59, 75; as lens for theological reflection, 62, 63, 79, 83, 97, 106; pattern in, 50–53, 66, 79; woman and the yeast (Luke 13:20-21), 53–57
permanent eschatology, 57
Pope Francis, 1, 48, 65, 82, 126, 128

Rausch, Thomas, 83

Reid, Barbara, 25, 53–55, 57, 82
resiliency, 27–28, 31
Rolheiser, Ronald, 89
Romero, Oscar, 92

sacramental worldview, 10–14, 16, 65, 91, 94. *See also* imagination
sacraments, 11, 13
Schilleebeckx, Edward, 58–61, 85, 100
Schrieter, Robert, 25
Schroeder, Roger, 95–96
Shea, Fr. Jack, 41
Snyder, Larry, 84
social analysis, 25–26, 42, 45, 70, 85, 86n1, 111
Socrates, 2, 31, 93
solidarity, 61, 62, 64, 66, 75, 83–86, 88, 91, 97–99, 123, 131
sources in theological reflection, 42, 44, 70; authority of experience, 45–46; context as source, 40, 45, 105, 115; experience as source, 33, 36, 44, 68; sacred texts and tradition as source, 44–45, 69, 113–14
spirituality defined, 88–90
spiritual practices, 88, 90, 93–94
St. Augustine, 14
styles of theological reflection, 24, 104; inculturation, 25; inter-religious, 26, 89, 113–14; liberative lens of women, 24–25, 29, 39, 83, 105; ministerial, 24, 28; practical, 25–26, 29; spiritual wisdom, 24, 27, 34
Sylvester, Nancy, IHM, 42

Tuckman, Bruce, 121

vocation, 91–93, 97, 100

Westley, Dick, 11, 83
Whitehead, James and Evelyn, 24, 28, 43, 47, 64, 65, 70, 85, 109
Woodard & Curran. *See* McKeown, Doug

About the Author

Christina R. Zaker, D.Min, is the director of Field Education and teaches in the Spirituality and Pastoral Ministry department at Catholic Theological Union. As a practical theologian, her main research and teaching areas focus on theological reflection as it intersects with the work of justice and ministry. She also focuses on spirituality especially in the context of families. Christina has published numerous articles in both peer-reviewed journals as well as mainstream magazines such as *US Catholic* and *National Catholic Reporter*.

She has spent over thirty years in teaching and ministry in a variety of settings including campus ministry at DePaul University, nonprofit work as the executive director of Amate House, the young adult volunteer program for the Archdiocese of Chicago, parish ministry, and deaconate formation. She is a frequent speaker and retreat director. Christina and her husband, Christopher, have four young adult children and live in Chicago.

www.ingramcontent.com/pod-product-compliance
Lightning Source LLC
Chambersburg PA
CBHW032215230426
43672CB00011B/2570